SWEATSHIRTS
with *Style*

OTHER BOOKS AVAILABLE FROM CHILTON

Robbie Fanning, Series Editor

SWEATSHIRTS
with Style

MARY MULARI

Chilton Book Company
Radnor, Pennsylvania

Designed by Anthony Jacobson
Photography by G. W. Tucker Photographic Studio
Illustrations by the author

Manufactured in the United States of America

Library of Congress Cataloging in Publication Data
Mulari, Mary.
    Sweatshirts with style / Mary Mulari.
        p.   cm.
    Includes bibliographical references and index.
    ISBN 0-8019-8392-4
    1. Sweatshirts.   2. Sewing.   3. Appliqué—Patterns.   I. Title.
TT649.M84   1993
746.9′2—dc20   93-8197
                                                            CIP

5 6 7 8 9 0   2 1 0 9 8 7 6 5 4

This book is dedicated, with love, to my mother, Helmi Koski.
As a child, I watched her sew many wonderful dresses for my sisters and me,
and she lit the spark of my sewing interest.

CONTENTS

FOREWORD

For a brief time I lived in Mary Mulari's neck of the woods in northern Minnesota. Mary and I met at, what else, a sewing seminar, and soon a friendship began. At lunch one day I distinctly remember Mary asking me for my opinion on appliqueing a sweatshirt. My response was, "A novel concept. . . ." Novel indeed! Little did I realize the impact Mary would have on my creative sewing, as well as the creative sewing of thousands of others.

Mary is an artist and her palette is fabric— in this instance, comfortable but basic sweatshirt fleece. After Mary's modifications and enhancements, the sweatshirt is anything but basic, yet still so comfortable. She has the rare ability to present designs that have clean lines and lots of style, making the sweatshirt truly wearable. Plus, her sewing techniques are simple, fun to sew, and often unique.

I have known Mary for many years, I have read all of her books, and I have seen her artistic expressions in fabric. She has unknowingly given me the license to be creative. I know her creativity and confidence will do the same for you.

Nancy Zieman

ACKNOWLEDGMENTS

It is important to me to say thanks to many individuals and companies that have helped with the ideas for this book. I appreciate the encouragement and support through all the years of developing new ways to make plain clothing better. Thanks to: Bernina of America, Coats & Clark, Concord Fabrics, Clotilde, Creative Beginnings, Creative Crystals, Dritz, Elna Inc., Handler Textile Corp., Hoffman California Fabrics, LaMode Buttons by B. Blumenthal, Liberty Fabrics Inc., Nancy's Notions, New Home Sewing Machine Co., C. M. Offray & Sons, Palmer/Pletsch, Pfaff American Sales Corp., Stretch & Sew Patterns, Sulky of America, Swiss-Metrosene, Therm O Web, Viking Sewing Machine Company, and VIP Fabrics.

In addition, many friends and sewing writers have shared their thoughts and suggestions. They include Gail Brown, Elizabeth Croy, Jackie Dodson, Robbie Fanning, Nancy Ward, and Nancy Zieman.

On a daily basis here in Aurora, Minnesota, I enjoy the encouragement and interest of many people who care about me and what I'm sewing or writing. Additional kind words, ideas, and support come each day through the mail and telephone from readers and students.

Thanks to all of you for your contributions to this book and to my life.

SWEATSHIRTS
with Style

1 Introduction

Does anyone remember life before sweatshirts? In the years since sweatshirts emerged from the locker room and gymnasium, it seems as if nearly everyone has discovered the joys of wearing these comfortable, soft garments. Like jeans, sweatshirts have become a wardrobe staple for all ages. You've probably heard someone you know say, "One of the best things about coming home from work or school is changing clothes and putting on my sweats." In my classes and seminars I've heard comments like "Sweatshirts—they're not just for phys. ed. class anymore" and "Everyone's wearing sweatshirts, even my grandmother at the nursing home; she likes the ones my mom decorates."

It makes sense to trim and personalize a piece of clothing that rates as everyone's favorite. The popularity of a sweatshirt only increases when you transform it into a personal creation, and there's no better way to express yourself and exercise your sewing talents.

Sweatshirts with Style is a collection of ideas for improving plain sweatshirts. The ideas are presented as **alterations**, or ways to change the basic construction of sweatshirts, and **decorations**, including sewing techniques and appliques.* I encourage you to look through the entire book to get an overview of the possibilities. By altering the structure of a sweatshirt, improving it with sewing techniques, or adding decorations to it, you can create a shirt that suits your style and fits better, too (Figure 1-1).

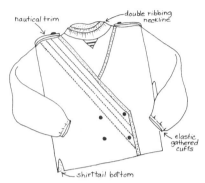
Fig. 1-1: A sweatshirt made stylish with various improvements

For most sweatshirts, the alterations should be completed before any decorations are added. Changes to the body of the garment will affect your choice and positioning of the decorations. In some cases, such as the sailor collar (Section 13), the alteration *becomes* the decoration.

Alter a sweatshirt not only to change its looks, but also to make it more useful. For example, some of the alterations in this book can be used to make a sweatshirt wearable by someone with a disability or other physical constraint. Con-sider the case of the girl who wears a back brace and finds that the sweatshirt's bottom ribbing rides up when she wears the shirt. Once she learns to remove the bottom ribbing and make the shirttail alteration (see Section 21), she can once again enjoy the comfort of "sweats."

If you decide not to alter your sweatshirt (don't make this rash decision without consulting Sections 9–22), go straight to the decorations sections (Sections 23–42) and let your imagination take over.

Many of the alterations and decorating ideas can be combined. By making several changes to one shirt, you will be able to disguise its ordinary sweatshirt appearance. Shirt A in Figure 1-2, for example, features a ruffled neckline (see Section 15), shirttail hemline (see Section 21), and elastic gathered sleeve ends (see Sections 20 and 22). In Shirt B, the waistline is gathered with a casing (see Section 20), and a collar and facings (see Section 10) trim the neckline. The sailor collar (see Section 13) and matching sleeve cuffs (see Section

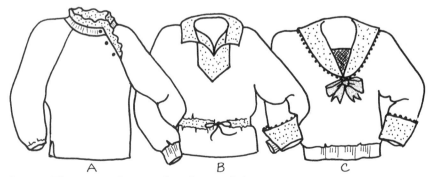
Fig. 1-2: Three sweatshirts, each with several changes

* When using this book, you'll notice that the word *applique* is written without an accent mark over the final "e." The French spelling of the word is *appliqué* (with the accent mark). Because of the word's common use and acceptance in the United States, I have chosen to spell the word without the accent mark.

22) change Shirt C from ordinary to extraordinary.

Look for the pattern guides (in sections where they are needed) on the pages following the instructions. Trace the guides from the book as you need them, and mark all the lines and notes shown on the patterns.

When thinking of sweatshirts to improve, don't limit yourself to the knit fleece garment that most people think of when they hear the word *sweatshirt*. I consider *sweatshirt* a generic term for any plain garment made better by sewing changes and trims. Use the ideas from this book for any piece of clothing that you can improve: a cotton sheeting shirt with short sleeves, a silk T-shirt, a corduroy jumper, or a tank top. With simple sewing or serging techniques, all of these "sweatshirts" can be made very special.

Let your own ideas direct you in your selections of sweatshirt changes. One of the most exciting aspects of working with sweatshirts is the unlimited number of possibilities available. You'll learn to use your personal taste and thoughts to make a sweatshirt whatever you want it to be. There are only a few rules, and you'll read them in Section 6, "Sweatshirt Changes: Choices and Decisions." Before you sew sweatshirts for other people, read "Designing Shirts for Others" (Section 7) and "Sweatshirt Ideas for Men and Boys" (Section 8).

Look at this book as a guide and a source of inspiration. Use it as a workbook near your sewing machine. If you'd like the pages to lie flat as you read and sew, take the book to a print shop and ask for a spiral binding to replace the current binding. Like the workbooks you may remember using in school, this book is intended to help you start and finish a sweatshirt project, guiding you along the way and giving you confidence to try new sewing techniques. You and I will both be very pleased if it also leads you to develop your own innovations and designs. Are you ready to begin?

PART ONE
GETTING STARTED

2 Supply List

Check the supply list before beginning any sewing project. Is there anything more frustrating than discovering, in the midst of sewing, that an essential "ingredient" is not available or within reach?

Sweatshirt. The first and most obvious item needed for a sweatshirt project is the sweatshirt itself. A purchased sweatshirt is one choice. It should be new or nearly new rather than worn and used. Consider the time and materials spent trimming the shirt; an already-worn-a-bit sweatshirt will look old after a few more washings even though the decorations will look new. You will have wasted your time. It is also wise to purchase quality sweatshirts, not "irregulars," for decorating, because the base garment should be worthy of your carefully crafted sewing additions. Also, look for sweatshirts with a fabic content of 50% (or more) cotton. The more natural fiber in the garment, the less "pilling" will occur.

Another option is to sew your own sweatshirt. Traditional styles and innovative new patterns are available, as are fleece fabrics with matching ribbing. You may want to sew the sweatshirt's front and back together at the shoulder seams before adding trims or alterations (Figure 2-1).

Fabrics and Assorted Trims. The next item on the list is fabrics

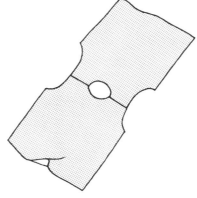

Fig. 2-1: Sew sweatshirt front and back together before decorating a shirt you sew.

for the alterations and trims. For most of the neckline alterations, ¼ yard (23cm) to ½ yard (46cm) will be an adequate amount. Although you may have plenty of selections in your fabric collection, there will be times when you'll want to buy a new fabric to coordinate with the colors of a special sweatshirt project. (You have my permission and encouragement to add to your fabric stash.) If you want the sweatshirt to be washable after you sew fabrics to it, make sure that the selected fabrics are washable. Besides cottons, think of the possibilities with corduroy, knits, denim, Ultrasuede, terrycloth, lace, and so on. All those pieces of ribbons and trims you have been saving can often be used on sweatshirts. Be sure to check the sewing room, your button and ribbon collections, and the box marked "Miscellaneous

Pieces of Neat Things for Sewing." See Section 5 for advice on pre-washing.

Thread. You will also need thread. Standard sewing thread (new and of good quality) is suggested for the techniques in this book, unless otherwise stated. For most of the sewing and applique, the thread color should match the fabrics or sweatshirt, though a contrasting color can add extra detail. Rayon and metallic threads work well for applique and other decorative stitching, and they offer additional interest to designs, too.

Sewing Machine Needles. Have plenty of new, high-quality sewing machine needles on hand. Generally, the size to use for sweatshirt projects is size 90 or 14. Because it is impossible to see machine needles growing dull or developing other problems, the best idea is to change the needle often and discard used needles. (Never be proud to say you have used the same needle for six months.)

Interfacing. Lightweight iron-on interfacing will be used for several neckline alterations. Most fabric additions to sweatshirts do not need to be crisp or stiff. In fact, "stable but soft" seems a good rule to follow in making additions to the garment compatible with the sweatshirt fabric. One of my favorite kinds of interfacing is a tricot knit with fusible backing. It provides adequate stability to lightweight cottons, and in addition, it stretches, as sweatshirt fleece does, in case you need to fuse a piece to the body of the garment.

Stabilizers. Many varieties of this important product are available. Stabilizers are used under the fabric for applique and other sewing, giving a firm, nonstretching surface for the sewing machine feed dogs to move the fabrics along. After sewing, the stabilizer is removed. Varieties include pin on (Pellon Stitch-N-Tear), iron on (Totally Stable Iron on Stabilizer), liquid (Perfect Sew), and water soluble (Solvy). Another choice very popular with many sewers is freezer paper. The shiny side can be fused onto the back of fabric. Experiment with the variety of stabilizers available. The advantage of using stabilizers like the liquid Perfect Sew or a water-soluble variety is that once the stitching is completed, the stabilizer is easily removed by soaking the garment in water. Press-on or pin-on stabilizers work well also, but it takes time—and a little patience—to pick off the stabilizer from the back of the stitching (wetting these stabilizers first is often helpful).

Basic Sewing Tools. The tools already in your sewing basket will be used frequently as you make changes to sweatshirts: scissors, pinking shears, pins, yardstick, 6″ (15cm) ruler, tape measure, and a seam ripper (Figure 2-2)—just in case!

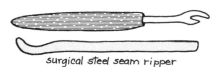

surgical steel seam ripper

Fig. 2-2: Two kinds of seam rippers

New Sewing Products. Newer additions to the basket will also be used.

Glue stick will temporarily hold two pieces of fabric together while you sew without pins. The glue will not gum up the sewing machine needle and washes out of the fabric when it is no longer needed. It does a great job of holding buttons in place so you can sew them to a garment. Just remember that it is not a permanent glue.

Fusible web from a bolt or a ¾″ (2cm) roll (Stitch Witchery) will permanently fuse fabrics together when placed between the fabrics and treated with the heat and pressure from an iron. This product provides a fast way to hem a garment.

Paper-backed fusible web such as Wonder-Under, Heat 'N Bond Lite, Trans-Web, and Aleene's Hot Stitch Fusible Web also offer time-saving help with applique. For specific directions, see the applique instruction in Part Three. I like to use this product to fuse trims and ribbons to a sweatshirt so they will stay in place while I sew them.

Washable marking pens and *chalk-markers* make easy-to-see lines to guide sewing, and afterward, the lines are easily removed.

Fray-stopping liquids such as Fray Check will seal the edges of cut fabric and ribbons, often eliminating sewing steps. It will be permanent and will dry clear on most fabrics. Treat a small area of the fabric or ribbon to test the product.

Sewing Equipment. Other tools such as rotary cutters and mats and tube-turning devices will be helpful as you produce sweatshirts with style.

The final addition to the sup-

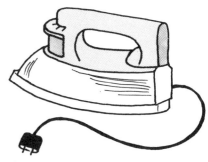

Fig. 2-3: An iron is essential.

ply and equipment list is the iron (Figure 2-3). With all sewing projects, the use of an iron is essential. My recommendation is that while the light on your sewing machine is on, the iron also should be on, and keep it nearby. An iron located three rooms away from the sewing machine will not be convenient to use often. Another piece of ironing and fusing equipment is a press, which applies heat and pressure to fabrics.

For frustration-free sewing, keep your supplies together and in an organized location. (Keeping it neat is a nice idea, but it's not required.) Knowing the approximate area to find the supplies you need will speed along the assembly and sewing, giving you extra time to produce more stylish sweatshirts (Figure 2-4).

Fig. 2-4: A sewing basket filled with supplies and equipment will make sewing a pleasant experience.

3 Sewing Machine Requirements

To create the sweatshirt alterations and trims presented in this book, you will need a sewing machine in good working condition. Give your machine some tender loving care by removing the dust from the bobbin area, adding oil if the manufacturer recommends it, and checking through the instruction manual for basic maintenance tips (Figure 3-1).

Most of the sewing will be straight stitching, but many of the decorative techniques, such as machine applique, require zigzag stitching. Decorative stitch patterns are another option for additional decoration (Figure 3-2).

If you begin a sweatshirt project and experience frustration with your machine's performance, take it to a reputable sewing machine dealer for a checkup. Trained repair professionals will often be able to locate and correct machine problems quickly. Working with a smooth-running sewing machine will bring back the pleasure to your sewing.

Fig. 3-2: Examples of decorative stitches

If machine problems persist, however, it may be time to consider buying a new sewing machine. Like a car, a sewing machine will not last through your lifetime. If you consider sewing an enjoyable hobby, you are entitled to have a dependable machine that produces professional results. Robbie Fanning has written that you "rise to the level of your tools. . . . If you love to sew, you deserve the best." ("You deserve the best." *The Creative Machine Newsletter*, Winter 1992, p 1).

If you are thinking of buying a machine, I recommend that you gather pieces of the fabrics you usually sew with and make a list of questions about features of sewing machines. Visit local sewing machine dealers with these fabrics and your list and take time to test-drive

the sewing machines. You will be amazed at the wonderful features. Ask about the availability of classes, machine maintenance, and repairs. These services should be considered as part of the decision of which machine to buy and where to buy it.

Though a serger is not required for the sweatshirt changes presented in this book, it can often speed up a project or offer an alternative way to complete a process. Serger uses are included and suggested when they are appropriate (Figure 3-3).

Although sewing machines are often used for practical purposes such as mending, their creative capabilities bring fun and personal satisfaction to sewing. Regard your sewing machine as a friend and partner in the creation of stylish sweatshirts.

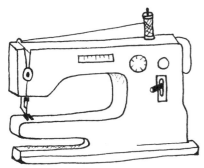

Fig. 3-1: Keep your sewing machine in good working condition.

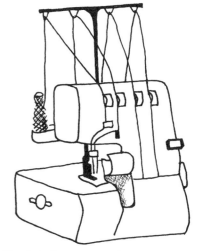

Fig. 3-3: A serger can increase your options.

4 Choosing a Sweatshirt

Now that sweatshirts are fashionable and appropriate for wear beyond the gymnasium, there are many choices and styles available for a sweatshirt project (Figure 4-1).

Crewneck sweatshirts with raglan sleeve styling (Figure 4-2) have been the basic style to use because they are readily available at a reasonable cost. Another basic style offers set-in sleeves with crewneck ribbing (Figure 4-3). Colors range from standard neutrals like gray and navy blue to currently fashionable and bright colors. Manufactur-

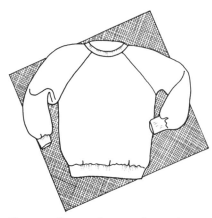

Fig. 4-2: Crewneck sweatshirt with raglan sleeves

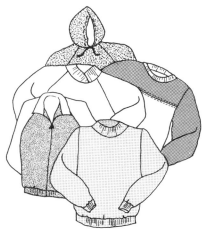

Fig. 4-1: Sweatshirt varieties

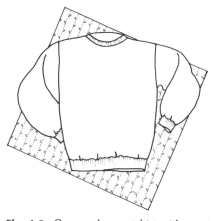

Fig. 4-3: Crewneck sweatshirt with set-in sleeves

ers continue to produce new and unique styles and colors so the possibilities for decorating ready-to-wear garments are endless.

The classic raglan and set-in sleeve styles are also found in other fabrics besides sweatshirt fleece. Cotton sheeting, rayon, silk, and lightweight knits are examples of alternate fabric garments which can be purchased or sewn with sweatshirt styling and then decorated. Lighter weight fabrics are preferred in warm climates or if your body thermostat finds sweatshirt fabric too hot to wear.

Both of the classic sweatshirt styles are available in patterns if you prefer to sew your own sweatshirts. The advantages of making your own garments are that you can make them really fit you and sew decorations to them while the fabrics are flat. Sweatshirt construction is a breeze with a serger, which also gives a ready-to-wear look to the seams.

With people of all ages adopting sweatshirts as their comfort garment, there's no doubt that sweatshirts are here to stay. Adding your own designer sewing touches makes them even more special.

5 Laundry Details: Prewashing and Long-Term Care

There's one important stop to make before you begin to sew on or assemble a sweatshirt, and that stop is the laundry room. Although you may feel reluctant to wash a

new garment or fabric, the process of prewashing is important to the future life of the garment.

Turn the sweatshirt inside out before laundering. This helps to

protect and preserve the outer fabric surface, which will be decorated. Launder by hand or in the automatic washer on a gentle cycle. Remember to be careful when laun-

Fig. 5-1: First stop: the laundry room

dering sweatshirts. There's already too much violence in the world; let's not bring it into the laundry room. The gentle cycle will ensure a long life for the sweatshirt before and after it is decorated.

Setting the color into the garment has been a concern and one of the reasons to prewash, particularly bright colored fabrics like red. Various recipes with salt or vinegar have come to me from the past when fabric dyes were made of natural substances. Vinegar or salt served to set the color into fabrics. Now that dyes are synthetic substances, these treatments no longer are effective. A study conducted by the University of Nebraska Textiles, Clothing and Design Department found no solutions to the problem of color running out of fabrics (Patricia Cox Crews, *Effectiveness of Dye Setting Treatments on Cotton Fabrics Dyed with Direct, Reactive, and Vat Dyes.* Lincoln, NE:

University of Nebraska, Journal Series #8562, Agricultural Research Division, 1989).

However, by prewashing, you will discover if the sweatshirt or sweatshirt fabric will lose color. One solution to a "bleeding" sweatshirt is to trim it with fabrics of darker colors. A white applique on a red sweatshirt that bleeds color will surely turn pink in the first washing.

What else should you prewash? Cotton and other washable fabrics used to decorate the shirt should be washed in advance. Besides revealing problems such as fading or excessive wrinkling, washing removes the sizing from fabrics and from fusible interfacing. (Sizing is known to dull needles.) Soak the interfacing in lukewarm water for 15 minutes. Rinse it thoroughly and allow it to air dry. Also wash

any ribbons and zippers that you plan to sew to sweatshirts.

It is best to hang up sweatshirts and let them air dry. At the least, limit the time they spin in the clothes dryer. By washing and drying a sweatshirt before you work on it, you also will set the size, eliminating future shrinkage.

After all the raw materials are dry, you're ready to begin sewing.

Once the sweatshirt is completed and ready to be worn, sold, or given as a gift, a care label is an important detail to add. A good way to ensure the longevity and good looks of a sweatshirt with style is to give it special care. (Hmmm . . . the same could be said for our bodies.) These laundering and care instructions should be written on a paper or fabric tag and included with each decorated sweatshirt you make (Figure 5-2).

For best results and a long life for this sweatshirt:

1. Turn the shirt inside out for laundering.
2. Hand wash if possible or wash by machine on a gentle cycle in lukewarm water.
3. Limit the time in the dryer to 5 minutes. Remove the shirt immediately, hang it, and let it air dry.
4. Press the shirt and all the decorations before you wear it.
5. Wear your sweatshirt in good spirits and good health.

Fig. 5-2: A sweatshirt care tag

6 Sweatshirt Changes: Choices and Decisions

The choices to be made regarding sweatshirt alterations and trims often take more time than the actual sewing. Even though the decision-making process may be

frustrating and time-consuming, it is of great importance to the end result, your own sweatshirt with style. Perhaps with the hints given in this section and throughout the

book, the choices will be easier for you to make and you'll be pleased with your creations.

Before you trim a sweatshirt, you will need to decide which alteration or design (or both) you'd like to use, as well as the fabric colors for the additions to the shirt and the location of the designs or alterations.

Focus first on any alterations to be made to the shirt. Plan the fabrics for the changes you will make, keeping in mind any decorations you plan to add later. Remember, the alterations are usually made first and then the decorations are added.

Along with the applique designs and trim ideas in this book, you may have a treasury of other designs. As you look through the possibilities, keep the alteration of the shirt in mind. For example, if it will become a cardigan (see Section 19), the appliques you sew onto the shirt will be placed on either or both sides of the new shirt front. It may be easier to decide on a design if you trace and cut the prospective designs from paper and play with them on the shirt. If the design has several parts, try rearranging the pieces so they are placed in a new order. This is part of the creativity of improving sweatshirts. By deciding on a design in a new formation or combining several ideas, you are giving the sweatshirt your individual, imaginative touch.

The size of the design is another aspect to consider. A large design will naturally draw more attention. Small designs can be repeated around the neckline or scattered over the shirt (Figure 6-1). How many designs should you use? Remember the rule that artists use in planning their work: An odd number is more pleasing to the eye than an even number.

Selecting fabrics and colors for the designs comes next. The sweatshirt color must be used as a basis for the additional fabrics. Also consider the fabric used for the alteration. You might want to repeat that fabric in the designs. Your fabric stash will be the first place to check for fabric possibilities. Look at the fabric combinations from a

Fig. 6-1: Repeat a small applique design around the neckline.

distance. Squint at them or take off your glasses. Do the colors blend with the shirt and each other or do they stand out? What effect do you want to produce with the colors? You'll be looking at both printed and solid color fabrics. Are the prints so busy that they draw attention away from the total design? Keep working with fabric combinations until the grouping looks right to you.

Where should the designs be placed on the sweatshirt? To avoid mistakes, it is essential to try on

the garment first. A shirt lying flat on a table takes on very different dimensions when put on a body, particularly a human female body. Take time to mark the bustline with straight or safety pins. Also mark the edge of the shoulders and the lines where the folds form between the shirt body and sleeves (Figure 6-2). Remove the shirt, pin on the designs where you think you want to sew them. Then try the shirt on again. This second time you'll be able to tell if the designs are placed so the effect is flattering.

This is my rule I hope you'll always follow: Try the shirt on *twice* before decorating and sewing. The first time you'll mark the bustline and shoulder areas and the second time, with the designs pinned on, you'll determine if the designs are in the right places. Never forget that any area you decorate is where the viewer's eye will be drawn when the shirt is worn. Taking time for two try-ons is the best insurance policy I know for placing decorations in the best locations.

A safe area for most women is above the bustline and around the

Fig. 6-2: Mark the bustline and shoulders to help you determine where to place designs.

shirt neckline so the viewer's eye is drawn from the design to the face. Another area that is often overlooked is the back of the sweatshirt. You won't be able to see the design while wearing the shirt, but others will. There are not many figure flaws on one's back, either.

The elements of design, color, and placement are equally important to the finished creation, and they deserve your careful consideration before you begin to decorate a sweatshirt.

7 Designing Shirts for Others

Once you have appeared wearing your own sweatshirt creation, your family and friends are sure to admire it and request one of their own. To share your creative work with special people is one of the pleasures of sewing. The challenge is . . . what to sew for your cousin, friend, brother, or work partner?

With a pen in hand, think about the man or woman who will receive your sweatshirt. Make a list of his favorite colors, hobbies, and collections. Think about her job and her personality. Writing the details will help you to focus on some potential ideas for decorations (Figure 7-1). Section 8 has more ideas for men.

Also consider the person's style in clothing. Does she dress in a conservative, subdued style? Are sparkling jewels and bright bold colors more her choice? Use what

you know about the person to "build" a creative sweatshirt appropriate to her personal taste.

You may be tempted or encouraged to create a special sweatshirt for someone's milestone birthday. Rather than sewing a large *40* on the front of the shirt, consider adding the number in a less conspicuous way so the sweatshirt will be worn after the birthday party is over. The number could be sewn onto a removable pocket (Figure 7-2) or embroidered above the sleeve cuffs.

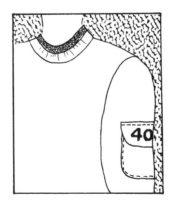
Fig. 7-2: Decoration idea for a milestone birthday

Do you and your cousin have a long-standing joke or favorite expression? Use the symbol of the joke as part of the sweatshirt decoration. Does your brother always forget your phone number? Embroider or machine stitch the num-

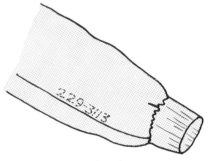
Fig. 7-3: Use an often-forgotten number as a decoration.

ber parallel to the sleeve seam above the wrist (Figure 7-3).

If you are making sweatshirts to sell, test the market by sewing a variety of shirt decorations. Pay attention to what's available and popular in ready-to-wear lines. While flowers are usually a safe design idea for women, be aware that many women prefer geometric shapes and other nonfeminine designs. Bright colors on white or black sweatshirts produce stunning garments, but not everyone will be attracted to bold statements. Plan to use some subtle colors and tone-on-tone color presentations to appeal to those who want understated decorations. The best advice is to be considerate of everyone's personal requirements for his or her clothing. We all have our own standards, and that's what makes the world an interesting place.

Fig. 7-1: Take time to make a list.

8 Sweatshirt Ideas for Men and Boys

As you look through this book, you will see many sweatshirt ideas for women and girls. If you're wondering what to do for men and boys, I have to be honest and encourage you to be cautious. What works for females often will not be acceptable to males. I'm interested in helping you use your valuable sewing time most productively to produce shirts for people who will appreciate and wear your creations. Some good trim ideas for men include a loop at the neckline for sunglasses (Section 41) and a chest pocket (Section 14), as shown in Figure 8-1.

The best advice regarding males and sweatshirts is to ask questions before decorating. My friend Nancy uses the rule that any male age four and older must be asked about possible sweatshirt renovations before she sews for that person.

Begin by analyzing the man's

or boy's preferences in ready-to-wear clothes. If his closet and drawers contain only traditional, safe colors, it would be wise to offer a sweatshirt idea in the same style. Classic shapes, like the argyle diamond, are likely to be acceptable trims (Figure 8-2).

Have an idea for something bold and different for a man you know? Present the idea to him, using the shirt and paper cutouts of the idea you have. If there's any hesitation in his response, try a different idea.

Design categories with possibilities for males include hobbies, sports, collections, and outdoor or nature designs. Logo designs sewn over the chest pocket of a shirt might be a satisfactory decoration.

Small monograms placed on the left side of a shirt are often acceptable trim. The initials can be made with the sewing machine or with waste canvas embroidery (see Section 32). I like to combine this detail with three rows of double-needle stitching across the chest of the shirt (Figure 8-3). This is not a bold decoration, but a style that has been appreciated and worn by many men.

This limited number of suggestions is not intended to discourage you from sewing decorated sweatshirts for males. Accept men (and women, too) for themselves, personal clothing styles included. Explain your sweatshirt ideas and listen to the response. Then sew.

Fig. 8-1: Fast and easy trims for a man's sweatshirt

Fig 8-2.: Classic argyle diamonds

Fig. 8-3: A simple decoration for a man's sweatshirt

PART TWO
SWEATSHIRT ALTERATIONS

9 Changing the Sweatshirt's Length

Ready-to-wear adult sweatshirts are usually cut for men's sizing, and as a result, many women find the fit to be awkward or uncomfortable. For short or short-waisted figures, the body of the sweatshirt is too long and the ribbing binds around the thighs or even near the knees. The sleeves may also be too long. Naturally, if you sew your own sweatshirt, you can make it to the correct length, but you might need this information for fixing that special vacation souvenir sweatshirt.

Fixing the length should be done before other decorations are begun. The first step is to try on the shirt to determine the amount of fabric to shorten or lengthen. Be cautious about the amount you decide to shorten the shirt, and remember to add a ¼" (6mm) seam allowance. If you cut away too much, you'll notice the problem, particularly in the back, when you wear the shirt.

Here are three methods for changing the length of a sweatshirt. The third method, fabric inserts, can also be used to lengthen a shirt if additional body or sleeve length is needed.

Moving the Bottom Ribbing

The first method of shortening is relocating the bottom ribbing. The basic procedure will be to remove the ribbing, cut a portion off the sweatshirt body, and then sew or serge the ribbing back onto the new bottom edge of the shirt.

1. First, decide how much of the sweatshirt you'd like to remove. Then, starting from the top of the ribbing and working up, measure that amount. Use a washable marking pen or chalk marker to mark this distance all around the shirt (Figure 9-1).

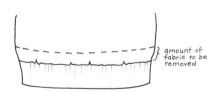

Fig. 9-1: Mark the sweatshirt.

2. Laying the shirt right side up, pull the ribbing away from the shirt body to expose the stitches that attach the two together. Insert the tip of the scissors or seam ripper under the threads and cut the stitches open all around the shirt (Figure 9-2). Even though there will be bits of thread and fuzz created by this cutting, I prefer this method of ribbing removal because it preserves the edges of both the ribbing and shirt body. Set the ribbing aside. Then cut off the excess body length, using the marks made in Step 1 as a cutting guide (Figure 9-3). Put the piece of extra sweatshirt material in your scrap box.

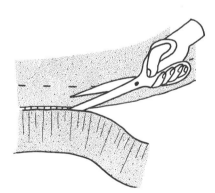

Fig. 9-2: Removing the ribbing

3. Use pins or a marking pen to mark the sides and center front and center back of both the ribbing and the new bottom edge of the sweat-

Fig. 9-3: Following your marks, cut away the extra length.

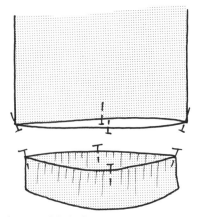

Fig. 9-4: Mark the quarter portions.

4. Using a ¼″ (6mm) seam allowance and polyester thread (because it stretches), sew or serge the ribbing and shirt body together. Sew with the ribbing on top. It is best to allow some give to the seam. A stretch stitch (Figure 9-5) on the sewing machine will allow the garment to stretch around the body without popping the seam. If your machine does not have stretch stitches, use a narrow zigzag stitch and pull slightly on the fabrics as you sew. Using a serger will allow you to attach the ribbing with ease and speed. Just remember to re-

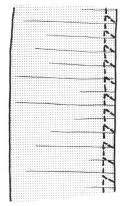

Fig. 9-5: Use a stretch stitch to reattach the ribbing.

move the pins before they reach the serger's knife edge. After sewing or serging the ribbing in place, press the seam flat and turn the ribbing down.

I refer to this shortening method as an invisible one because it does not change the appearance or structure of the sweatshirt. The important difference will be in the way that the shirt fits.

Sewing Tucks

The second method of shortening is to sew in tucks around the body of the sweatshirt, which will add a subtle trim (Figure 9-6). Determine the excess length of the shirt to decide on the number and size of the tucks. Remember that a tuck will reduce the shirt's length by twice the measurement of the front of the tuck. For example, a ½″ (1.3cm) tuck actually takes up 1″ (2.5cm) of fabric.

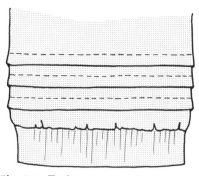

Fig. 9-6: Tucks sewn into the sweatshirt body

1. Measure up from the top of the ribbing to the place where you wish the fold of the lowest tuck to end up (Figure 9-7). A good distance might be 3″ (7.5cm). Plan the tuck fold locations by pinning tucks into the shirt as a trial to determine the placement and distance apart from one another. Try on the shirt to test the tuck locations and new shirt length. Mark the tuck foldlines all around the shirt.

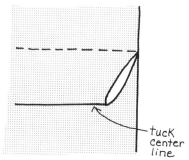

Fig. 9-7: The center of the tuck is actually the foldline.

2. Get ready to sew by folding the bottom of the sweatshirt up and inside (wrong sides together) until you form the fold on the lowest tuck center line (Figure 9-8). Pin this fold securely all around the shirt. Sew around the shirt to form the tuck at the width you have chosen. For example, use the ½″ (1.3cm) guide on the machine if you want a ½″ tuck. A straight machine stitch and a standard stitch length can be used.

3. Fold the sweatshirt bottom up farther to form the center-line folds for additional tucks. Pin the tucks in place and sew in the same man-

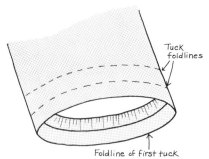

Fig. 9-8: Preparing to sew the first tuck

ner. After all the tucks are sewn, press them down toward the bottom of the shirt (see Figure 9-6).

The tucks form a dimensional but subtle trim at the bottom of the sweatshirt and serve the purpose of shortening the shirt as well.

Adding Fabric Inserts

Method three is the addition of fabric inserts to shorten or lengthen the sweatshirt. An insert can be a strip of fabric to match the sweatshirt color (the most subtle choice), a band of Seminole patchwork (see Section 29), a piece of fleece in a contrasting color, or any fabric as washable and durable as the sweatshirt (Figure 9-9).

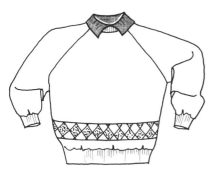

Fig. 9-9: A fabric insert sewn into a sweatshirt

Materials Needed

- ¼ yard (23cm) fabric for each insert

1. Measure up from the top of the ribbing to the place where you want the bottom of the insert fabric to be. For example, try 2″–3″ (5–7.5cm) up from the ribbing. Mark this line around the shirt.

2. Determine the length of the fabric insert by measuring around the

sweatshirt body on the line of marks from Step #1. Decide on the width of the insert (see Steps #5 and #6 to help with this decision). Add ½″ (1.3cm) to the length and width measurements for seam allowances. Cut the insert from fabric and sew or serge the ends right sides together to form a tube. Use ¼″ (6mm) seams for all seams in this method (Figure 9-10).

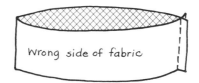

Fig. 9-10: A fabric insert with ends sewn together

3. Insert the scissors tip through the shirt on one of the marks from Step #1, and cut carefully around the shirt following the marks. You have now cut the sweatshirt into two sections (Figure 9-11).

Fig. 9-11: Sweatshirt ready for a fabric insert

4. Pin the bottom edge of the fabric insert to the cut edge of the bottom section of the shirt, right sides together. Position the seam of the insert at one side of the shirt body.

Sew or serge the insert onto this part of the shirt (Figure 9-12).

Fig. 9-12: The fabric insert is sewn to the lower portion of the sweatshirt first.

5. To shorten the sweatshirt, you need to cut away a portion of the upper part of the shirt. It is important to cut a piece from the shirt that is *wider* than the fabric insert. For example, if the shirt insert is 4″ (10cm) wide, you might cut away 5″ (12.5cm) or 6″ (15cm) of the shirt body. The difference in width determines how much shorter the "new" sweatshirt will be. After cutting, sew or serge the top edge of the insert to the top section of the shirt, right sides together.

6. To lengthen the sweatshirt, the upper edge of the insert will be sewn or serged directly to the *edge* of the upper shirt section without removing any of the shirt fabric, as the shortening procedure requires. Thus, the width of the insert determines how much longer the "new" sweatshirt will be.

All three length-changing methods can also be applied to sweatshirt sleeves.

When you plan to sew for others, remember to suggest length alteration as a possibility. When you take the time to change a sweatshirt's length, you tailor a ready-to-wear garment, making it more comfortable to wear.

13

10 Collar with Facings

With the addition of two facings and a collar, the sweatshirt front opens to a "v." One of the facings shows on the shirt front, the other lines the back of the opening, and the collar is sewn to the top of the neck ribbing (Figure 10-1). Facing and collar patterns for both adults and children can be found within this section (Patterns 10-1 through 10-3). Additional collar ideas, including a sailor collar and turtlenecks, are given in the sections that follow (see especially Sections 11, 12, 13, and 18).

Fig. 10-1: A collar and facings create an open, comfortable neckline.

Conventional Collar with Facings

Materials Needed:

- ⅔ yard (61cm) woven fabric for facings and collar
- ¼ yard (23cm) lightweight fusible interfacing

1. Trace the collar and facing patterns from this section. Note the choice of squared, pointed, or curved edges for both the collar and facings. Cut two facings from fabric and mark the stitching and center front lines on the wrong side of the inside facing. Serge or zig-zag stitch around the sides and bottom edges of the inside facing. Mark the center line on the right side of the outside facing (Figure 10-2). Turn under and press ½" (1.3cm) along the sides and bottom edges of the outside facing. For an even curved edge at the bottom, use a pocket corner template or make a lightweight cardboard pattern of the curved edge and press the seam allowance over the pattern.

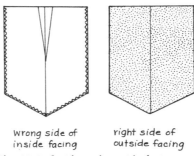

Wrong side of inside facing   right side of outside facing

Fig. 10-2: Inside and outside facings with marking lines and stitching

2. On the sweatshirt front, draw the center line with a washable marker from the neck ribbing to the middle of the shirt. Position the two facings with right sides together, putting the inside facing (the one with the stitched or serged edge) on top. Place them at the top of the shirt front, matching the center lines of the facings and the shirt (Figure 10-3).

3. Sew the facings to the shirt, following the "v" stitching line drawn on the top facing. Sew one tiny stitch across the bottom point of

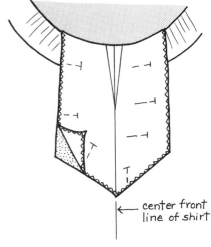

center front line of shirt

Fig. 10-3: Pin the facings to the top of the shirt front.

the "v" (Figure 10-4). Cut carefully along the center line from the neckline edge through the shirt and facings to the point of the "v." Turn the top facing to the inside of the shirt. Press the seam line.

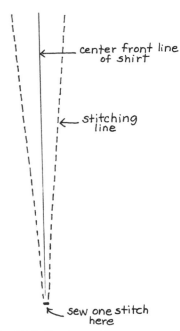

center front line of shirt

stitching line

sew one stitch here

Fig. 10-4: Sewing guide

4. Pin the two facings and sweatshirt together. You will notice that the inside facing extends beyond the edge of the pressed back edge of the outside facing. When you sew the facings and shirt together by stitching on the outside facing, you will also be sure of sewing and catching the inside facing (Figure 10-5). Sew about ⅛″ (3mm) from the edge of the outside facing through the sweatshirt and inside facing. This alteration is half done, and now you are ready to add the collar.

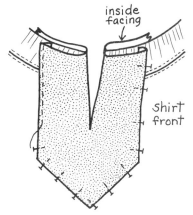

Fig. 10-5: Sew the facings onto the shirt.

5. Measure around the top edge of the neckline ribbing with a tape measure on its edge, for a more accurate measurement (Figure 10-6). Do not pull or stretch out the ribbing while measuring. Add ½″ (1.3cm) to the measurement for seam allowances. Compare half this measurement to the length of the neck edge of the collar pattern. Note that the collar pattern is only half a collar and that the foldline is to be moved to fit the desired

Fig. 10-6: Use the tape measure on its edge.

length. Cut two collars. Fuse interfacing to the wrong side of one collar.

6. Place the two collar pieces with right sides together. Sew around all the edges but the neck edge of the collar, a ¼″ (6mm) seam allowance (Figure 10-7). Trim the seam allowance and turn the collar so right sides are out. Press.

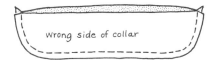

wrong side of collar

Fig. 10-7: Sew the two collar pieces together.

7. Turn the sweatshirt inside out. Fit and pin the right side of the neck edge of the collar piece without interfacing to the wrong side of the neck ribbing. Use a ¼″ (6mm) seam allowance and sew the collar to the shirt (Figure 10-8). Turn back ¼″ (6mm) along the edge of the other collar piece, press, pin, and hand sew into place on the right side of the neck edge. (For those of you reluctant to sew by hand: Hand stitching will not take long and will be the neatest way to attach the second piece of the collar.)

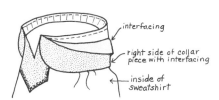

interfacing

right side of collar piece with interfacing

inside of sweatshirt

Fig. 10-8: Sewing the collar to the neck ribbing

8. You may choose to complete this neckline treatment by topstitching around the collar edge and the "v" opening (Figure 10-9).

Adding a collar to the neckline spreads the facings apart when the shirt is worn. This will offer a comfortable, open neckline, preferred by many people.

Fig. 10-9: Topstitching adds a finishing touch.

Options:

If you want the collar ends to meet to hold the facing sides together, add ties or a button-and-loop closure at the neckline (Figure 10-10).

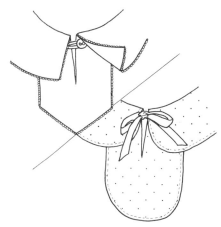

Fig. 10-10: Two ways to hold the collar closed

Narrow trim or lace can be sewn around the collar and outer edges of the front facing. Use glue stick to apply the trim and hold it in place while you sew.

Fabric used for the front facing or the collar can be given texture by the addition of sewn tucks (see Section 9), double-needle stitching (see Section 27), or Seminole patchwork (see Section 29). Add such features to the fabric before you cut out the facing and collar pieces (Figure 10-11).

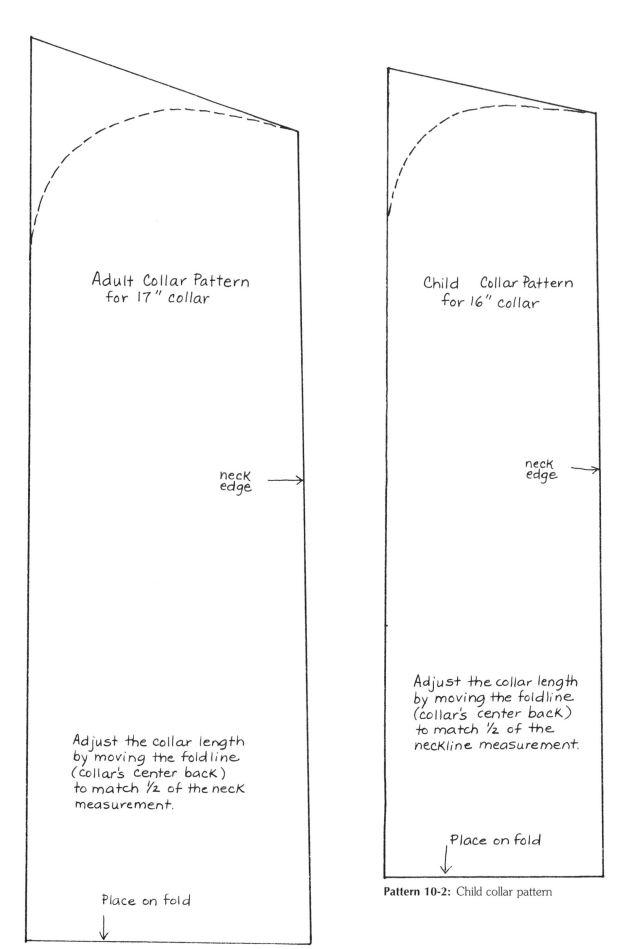

Adult Collar Pattern
for 17" collar

neck
edge →

Adjust the collar length
by moving the foldline
(collar's center back)
to match ½ of the neck
measurement.

Place on fold
↓

Pattern 10-1: Adult collar pattern

Child   Collar Pattern
for 16" collar

neck
edge →

Adjust the collar length
by moving the foldline
(collar's center back)
to match ½ of the
neckline measurement.

Place on fold
↓

Pattern 10-2: Child collar pattern

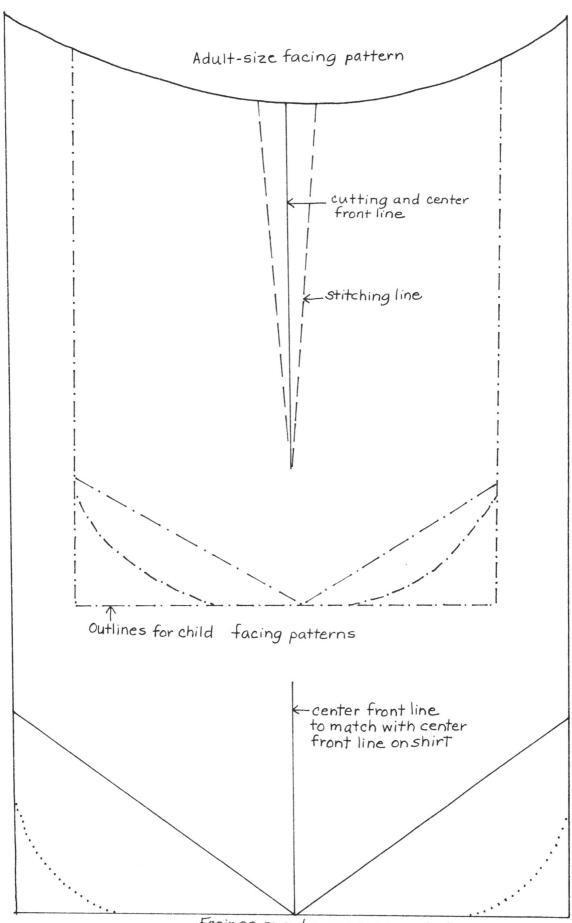

Adult-size facing pattern

cutting and center front line

stitching line

Outlines for child facing patterns

center front line to match with center front line on shirt

Facings may be square, rounded, or pointed at the bottom edge.

Pattern 10-3: Patterns for adult and child facings

Fig. 10-11: Tucks give another dimension to this neckline treatment.

Collar with Facings Using Neckline Trim

Using an idea from ready-to-wear lines, this method of attaching the collar includes a band of fabric or purchased trim to add extra detail (Figure 10-12). This method can also be used with other altera-

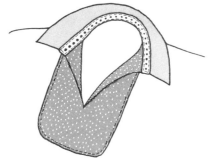

Fig. 10-12: A piece of ribbon or decorative braid can cover the neck edges.

1. Follow Step #1 through Step #6 of the instructions for a conventional collar with facings.

2. With the under collar meeting the right side of the sweatshirt neck edge, pin the collar to the neckline. Serge or sew the collar onto the

tions such as the neckline placket (see Section 14) and the cardigan (see Section 19).

shirt, using a narrow seam allowance of ⅛″ (3mm), as shown in Figure 10-13.

Fig. 10-13: Sew the neck edges of both collar pieces to the ribbing.

3. Cut a piece of decorative trim, fabric, or bias tape slightly longer than the collar edge sewn to the shirt. Pin or fuse the trim in place over the seam that attaches the collar to the shirt. Fold under the ends of the strip to make a neat cover for the raw edges of the collar and shirt. Sew along the edges of the trim strip to attach it to the shirt.

11 Cowl Collars

Replace the neck ribbing on a plain sweatshirt with a larger neck opening and a casual cowl collar. Add a drawstring to the collar for

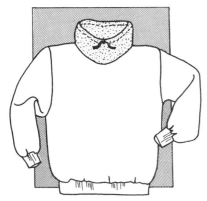

Fig. 11-1: A cowl collar with a drawstring

extra detail. Select print or solid-color fabrics such as woven cottons or knits with a soft drape (Figure 11-1). Here are instructions for two kinds of cowl collars, stand-up and draped.

Stand-up Cowl

Materials Needed:

■ ¼–½ yard (23cm–46cm) fabric

1. Measure and mark 1″ (2.5cm) below the neck ribbing all around the neckline. Staystitch with a straight stitching line around the neckline on the marks. The stitching will help retain the shape of the neckline (Figure 11-2).

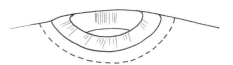

Fig. 11-2: Staystitch around the neckline.

2. Cut away the ribbing and sweatshirt fabric slightly less than ¼″ above the stitching line.

3. Measure the distance around the staystitching by using a tape measure on its edge, for a more accurate measurement. Add ½″ (1.3cm) to the measurement for seam allowances. Cut the collar fabric to this length and 8″ (20.5cm) wide. (With 8″ [20.5cm] of fabric, approximately 4″ [10cm]

will be the finished collar's width. Adjust the measure for a taller or shorter cowl collar.)

Steps for adding a drawstring casing follow. If you don't want to add one, skip ahead to Step #6.

4. Fold the collar fabric in half by length and width (Figure 11-3).

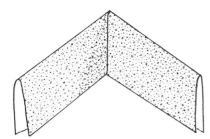

Fig. 11-3: Fold and press the collar fabric.

Press these folds for use as guides and then open the fabric flat again.

5. For a casing at the top of the collar, sew in a ½″ (1.3cm) long buttonhole on line B, directly below line A (Figure 11-4). If you plan to sew the casing lower on the collar, plan the distance from line A and sew the buttonhole on line B. Line B marks the collar's center front.

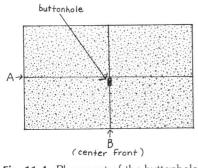

Fig. 11-4: Placement of the buttonhole

6. Stitch the short sides of the collar fabric right sides together with a ¼″ (6mm) seam allowance (Figure 11-5). Press the seam open. Fold the collar tube in half lengthwise, matching the long edges. The wrong sides of the fabric will be inside the fold (Figure 11-6). Baste the edges together. Now the collar is ready to be sewn to the sweatshirt.

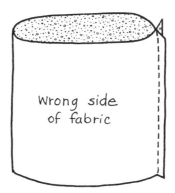

Fig. 11-5: Sew the sides of the collar fabric together.

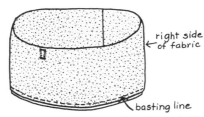

Fig. 11-6: Fold cowl collar tube in half.

7. Place the seam line of the collar at the center back of the shirt. With the right side of the collar to the right side of the sweatshirt, pin the basted edge of the collar to the neckline. Sew or serge the collar to the shirt, using a ¼″ (6mm) seam allowance. Press the seam. Topstitch the seam allowance to the shirt body below the collar (Figure 11-7). This is another idea borrowed from ready-to-wear.

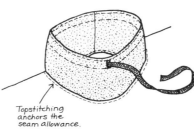

Fig. 11-7: After sewing the collar to the neckline, press the seam allowance toward the shirt and topstitch the seam allowance to the shirt body. Then the casing is sewn.

8. To make the drawstring casing, pin together the two sides of the fold at the top of the collar. Sew a casing by topstitching through both layers of the collar along the edge of the collar, just above the buttonhole. To complete the casing, stitch along the collar just below the buttonhole. Thread a ribbon, braid, or fabric tube through the casing to add the drawstring as shown in Figure 11-7.

Draped Cowl

Another type of cowl is one that extends lower on the garment than the stand-up cowl does. This collar is best made from a soft, drapey fabric such as interlock knit or rayon challis (Figure 11-8).

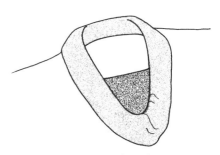

Fig. 11-8: The draped cowl

1. The rounded neckline pattern is found within this section (Pattern 11-1). Trace the shape from the book and then trace it on the center front of the shirt.

2. Staystitch along the pattern line on the shirt and around the shirt back neckline directly below the neck ribbing. The staystitching helps stabilize the sweatshirt neckline. Trim away the ribbing and sweatshirt fabric by cutting slightly less than ¼″ (6mm) from the staystitching line (Figure 11-9).

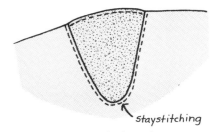

Fig. 11-9: Staystitch along the pattern line and below the back neck ribbing.

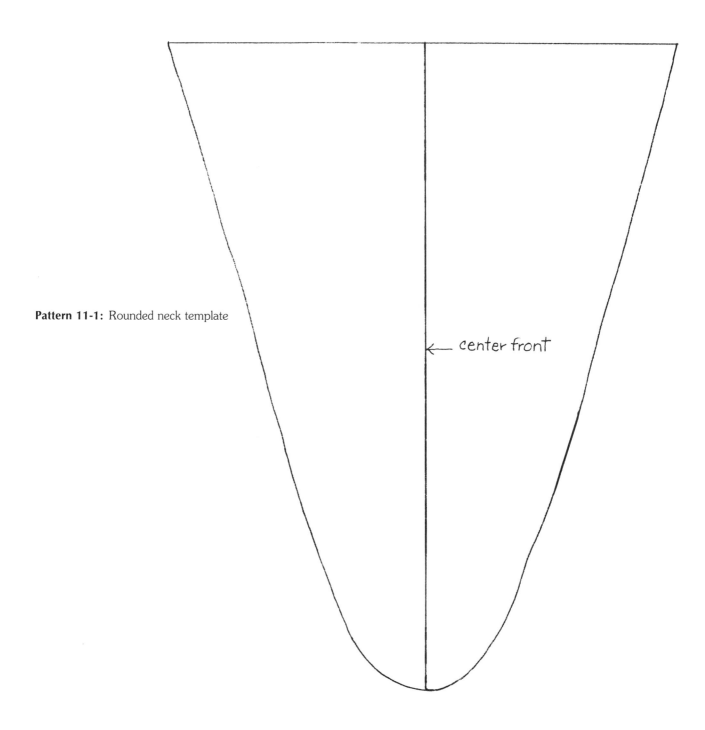

Pattern 11-1: Rounded neck template

← center front

3. Proceed with the directions provided in Steps 3, 6, and 7 for the stand-up cowl, except cut the cowl fabric 12″ (30.5cm) wide instead of 8″ (20.5cm).

4. To avoid making this large cowl opening too revealing, you will want to add an insert fabric inside the neckline across the shirt front (Figure 11-10). The insert detail also adds interest and holds the col-

Fig. 11-10: A fabric insert inside the neckline

lar sides together. The best way to plan and cut the insert will be to try on the shirt after the collar is attached. Place and pin the top straight edge of Pattern 11-1 at the level at which you want to place the fabric insert. Take the shirt off.

5. Trace the curve of the cowl neckline onto the paper pattern. This will form a pattern guide. Remove the paper from the neckline and draw a line ½″ (1.3cm) from the first line you drew (Figure 11-11). Cut the pattern along this line.

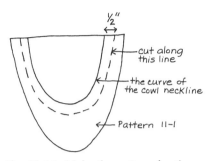

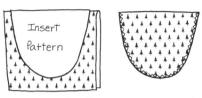

Fig. 11-11: Make the pattern for the insert.

6. Fold the fabric selected for the insert, wrong sides together. Place the straight edge of the insert pattern on the fold. Cut the insert, which will be of two layers of fabric. Leave the insert fabric folded. Serge finish or zigzag the edges together (Figure 11-12).

Fig. 11-12: Cut the insert pattern and serge or sew around the cut edges.

7. Sew the insert in place in the neckline or sew pieces of Velcro to both the sweatshirt neck and the insert so you can change the insert. (What a good idea!)

12 Knit Collars and Turtlenecks

Sew a knit collar or turtleneck ribbing into the crew neck of a sweatshirt and create the look of layered garments. Although many people like the look of layered clothing, not everyone can tolerate the weight or warmth of layers. (This is hard to believe for those of us who live in northern Minnesota.)

These additions to the neckline are easy to do (Figure 12-1).

Knit collars are available in fabric stores and through mail-order sources. The collars are made in adult and children's lengths, so test the collar to make sure it will stretch around the head of the wearer.

Knit Collar

Materials Needed:

■ purchased knit collar

1. Once you have a collar for this project, it's a good idea to test it inside the neckline before sewing it in place. Pin the raw edge of the collar to the wrong side of the neckline. Overlap the two ends of the collar at center front and over the ditch where the neck ribbing and shirt body meet (Figure 12-2).

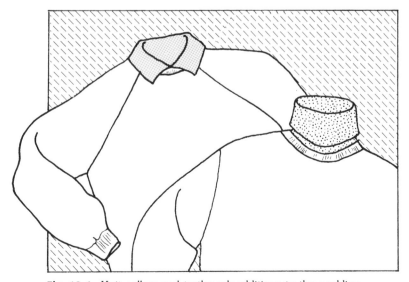

Fig. 12-1: Knit collars and turtleneck additions to the neckline

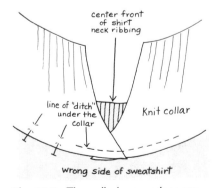

Fig. 12-2: The collar's raw edges are pinned over the ditch inside the shirt neckline and the ends are overlapped.

Make sure the center line of the collar is at the center back line of the neckline. After pinning the entire collar in place, inspect the results.

- Does the collar seem too long or large? Overlap the ends a greater amount at center front. The collar ends will spread apart and look natural when the collar is folded over the ribbing.

- Does the collar width seem too short when it is folded over the ribbing? You may prefer to remove the neck ribbing, cut it to make it narrower, and reattach it before sewing on the collar.

- Do you have to stretch the collar a great amount to fit it into the neckline? The collar you are using may be too short for the shirt. Try a different, longer collar. A *bit* of stretching of the collar is not a problem.

2. After the collar is adjusted to fit inside the neckline, repin the collar through the garment's right side. Make sure that the bottom edge of the collar extends slightly past the ditch between the ribbing and the shirt. This will guarantee that the stitching, which will be done from the right side of the shirt, will catch the collar.

3. Attach the collar to the shirt by sewing on the right side of the shirt in the ditch. The top thread color should match the shirt and the bobbin thread color should match the collar. If possible, sew with a straight stretch stitch (two stitches forward and one stitch back). This stitch builds stretch into the neckline so the seam will not pop when the neck opening is stretched over a head. By stitching in the ditch, you will add an invisible seam line to the garment neckline (Figure 12-3).

If your sewing machine does not have stretch stitches, adjust to a short straight stitch length and pull slightly on the garment and

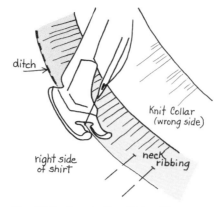

Fig. 12-3: Sew in the ditch with a stretch stitch.

collar as you sew. This procedure will also give stretching capabilities to the new neckline.

Option:

Another way to position a collar in the neckline is to place the collar opening in line with the raglan seam (Figure 12-4).

Fig. 12-4: The collar opening also can be placed at the raglan seam.

Turtleneck

Materials Needed:

■ 12″ (30.5cm) ribbing fabric

The process of adding a turtleneck to a sweatshirt is similar to adding a knit collar but requires first that you sew a tube of ribbing fabric to create the neck piece addition.

1. To determine the size of the knit ribbing fabric needed for your sweatshirt's turtleneck, measure the neck piece of a turtleneck shirt that fits well or use the guidelines that follow. The width of the ribbing will

be 10″ (25.5cm) to 12″ (30.5cm) for an adult. Of course, you are welcome to alter this measurement. With the tape measure on its edge, measure around the ditch, or seamline, attaching the crewneck ribbing to the sweatshirt. Use two-thirds of this measurement as a guide for the length of the ribbing. (Not good with math? Simply fold the tape measure amount into three equal segments and read the measurement at the second fold of the tape (Figure 12-5). Before cutting, stretch this amount of ribbing around your head to make sure the turtleneck tube will fit. Then cut the ribbing to your chosen dimension.

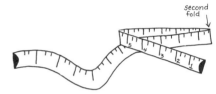

Fig. 12-5: After measuring around the neckline of the sweatshirt, fold the tape measure into three equal parts and read the measurement at the second fold to easily determine two-third's of the measurement.

2. Bring the right sides of the ribbing fabric together and sew or serge the fabric into a tube (Figure 12-6). Use a ¼″ (6mm) seam allowance. Press. Turn the fabric right side out.

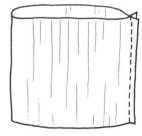

Fig. 12-6: Sew or serge the ribbing into a tube, right sides together.

3. Fold the tube in half lengthwise by meeting the raw edges, with the right side of the fabric on the outside (Figure 12-7). Mark the center front of the ribbing tube so it can

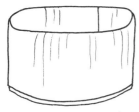

Turtleneck - right side
of fabric

Fig. 12-7: Fold the ribbing tube in half lengthwise.

be matched up with the center front of the sweatshirt neckline.

4. Keeping all pins on the outside of the shirt, pin the ribbing tube's raw edges inside the sweatshirt neckline, right side of ribbing to wrong side of sweatshirt. The edges should extend past the ditch to ensure catching them in the

seam. Place the seamline of the ribbing tube at the center back of the shirt. The *center* front of the turtleneck ribbing should be matched to the *center* front of the neckline. Pin the rest of the ribbing piece in place in the neckline.

5. Stitch the turtleneck onto the shirt as explained in Step #3 of the knit collar instructions. You will stitch in the ditch with a straight stretch stitch. Use top thread to match the sweatshirt and bobbin thread to match the ribbing.

Option:

Miniature turtlenecks, a variation of this procedure, can be used to add accent colors or to fill-in a neckline that is too large. Add one

or two extra ribbings to show just above the original crew neckline (Figure 12-8). Remember this idea when you find that the neckline of a favorite sweatshirt has stretched out of shape. Another band of ribbing added to the neck might make it look better. If you receive a sweatshirt as a gift and find it's not your best color, add a better color of ribbing to the neckline and then use that same color in other trim for the shirt.

Fig. 12-8: Miniature turtlenecks extending slightly above the original neck ribbing

13 Sailor Collar

The traditional styling of a sailor collar adds casual, classic appeal to a sweatshirt. The same collar idea can be adapted for a variety of looks, such as a feminine, lace-trimmed version (Figure 13-1).

Fig. 13-1: Sailor collar versions

Materials Needed:

- 1 yard (.92m) woven fabric for collar
- ¼ yard (23cm) for contrasting fabric trim
- 30" (76cm) bias tape or bias fabric strip

1. Trace the two pieces of the collar pattern on the next two pages (Patterns 13-1 and 13-2). Tape the two pieces together at the shoulder seams, as indicated on the pattern. To test the entire pattern on the shirt neckline, trace the taped pattern onto a folded piece of tissue or pattern tracing paper, being sure to place the back center of the collar on the fold (Figure 13-2). Cut a complete collar pattern from the paper. Pin the pattern around the neckline and down the front of the shirt to see how it

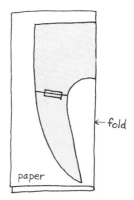

Fig. 13-2: Tape the two collar sections together and place them on folded paper.

will be positioned. Try the shirt on with the pattern pinned in place. Make any adjustments to the pattern before cutting it from fabric.

2. Place the collar pattern on a double layer of fabric and cut two collars. With right sides of the fab-

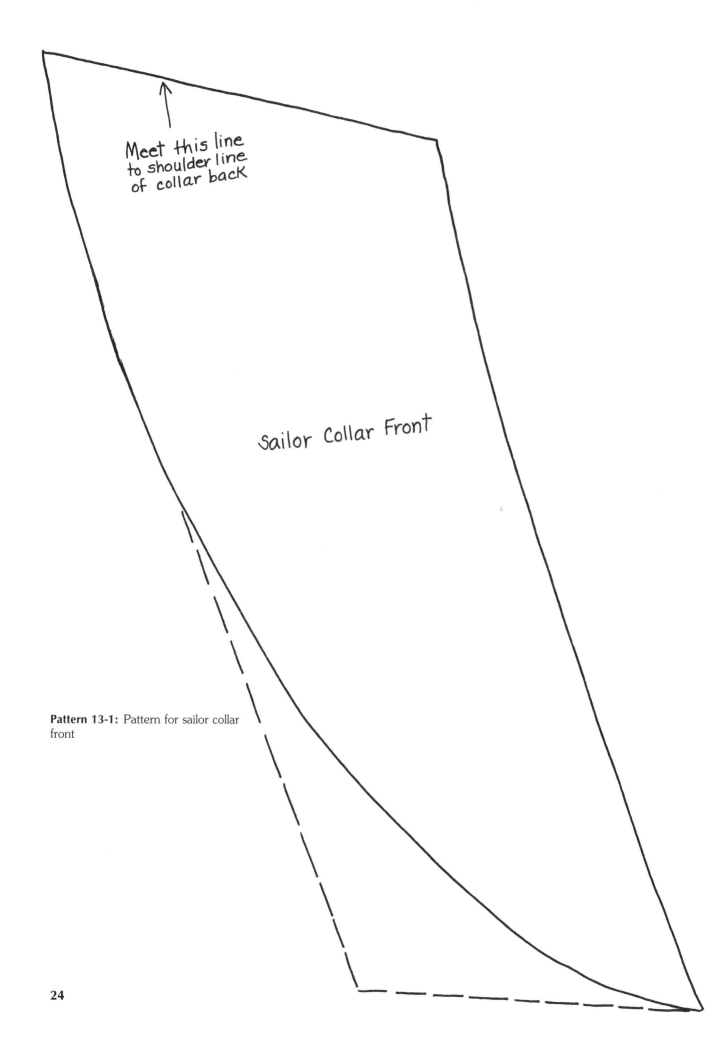

Meet this line
to shoulder line
of collar back

Sailor Collar Front

Pattern 13-1: Pattern for sailor collar front

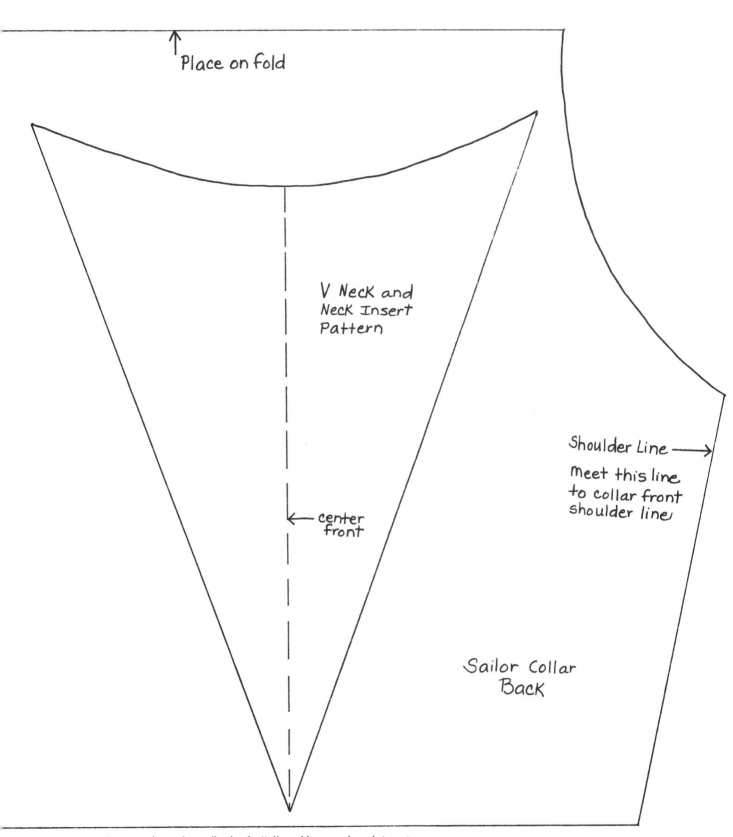

Place on fold

V Neck and
Neck Insert
Pattern

← center
front

Shoulder Line ⟶

meet this line
to collar front
shoulder line

Sailor Collar
Back

Pattern 13-2: Patterns for sailor collar back, ''v'' neckline, and neck insert ric together, sew around the outer sides and back of the collar pieces (Figure 13-3). Trim and clip the seams and corners. Turn the collar right side out and press.

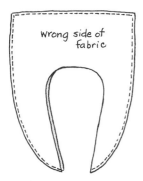

Fig. 13-3: Sew two collar pieces together with right sides of the fabric together.

3. Add trim such as middy braid or soutache braid around the collar now. Use a glue stick to hold the trim in place as you sew. Position the braid ¾" (2cm) away from the collar edge (Figure 13-4). Use a narrow zigzag stitch for wider braid or a straight stitch in the center ditch of a narrow soutache braid. Lace can also be added around the outer edges of the collar by using the glue stick to hold it in place. (This is one of my favorite uses of the glue stick because it eliminates the need for pins, which are often in the way of the presser foot. Also, when pins are removed, the trim or ribbon may move.)

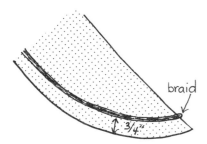

Fig. 13-4: Adding a braid to the collar

4. Find the v-neck template guide on the previous page (Pattern 13-

2) and trace it onto paper. Cut the pattern from the paper and pin it on the shirt front, lining up the template's center front line with the shirt's center front (Figure 13-5). Draw the sides of the "v" on the shirt with a washable marker or chalk marker. Lay the completed collar around the neck and on the diagonal lines of the "v". If necessary, adjust the lines of the "v" to fit the collar. Save the paper template.

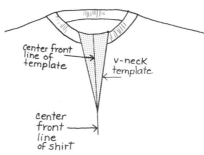

Fig. 13-5: Line up the center front lines on the shirt and the template.

5. Staystitch the neckline by sewing around the back of the sweatshirt neck directly below the ribbing and on the "v" lines on the front of the shirt. Cut off the ribbing and shirt fabric ¼" (6mm) inside the staystitching line (Figure 13-6).

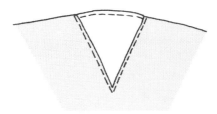

Fig. 13-6: Cut away the shirt fabric and ribbing.

6. Pin the collar into the neck opening. Begin by pinning the center back of the collar to the center back of the shirt, with the wrong side of the collar against the right side of the shirt. Meet the collar ends at the bottom of the "v" on the shirt. The collar ends may ex-

tend past the end of the "v" (Figure 13-7). Sew the collar to the shirt with a ¼" seam allowance.

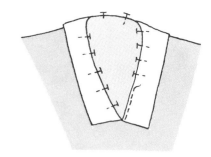

Fig. 13-7: Pin the collar to the neckline and sew along the edge.

7. Use a 30" (76cm) strip of bias tape or a bias strip of fabric 1" (2.5cm) wide and place it right side down over the neckline edge of the collar. Pin it in place (Figure 13-8). Sew it onto the collar and shirt with a ¼" (6mm) seam allowance. Trim the seam allowance, cutting through the sweatshirt, collar, and bias tape.

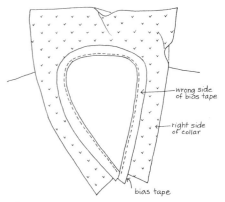

Fig. 13-8: Sew the bias strip around the neckline.

8. Press the bias strip over the seam and turn the edge of the strip to the inside of the sweatshirt. Machine sew this edge of the bias strip to the garment (Figure 13-9).

9. Now it's time to decide the size and position of the fabric insert between the sides of the collar. The easiest way to do this is to try on the shirt and use the v-neck paper

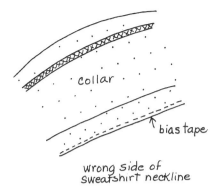

Fig. 13-9: The bias strip covers the seam around the neckline.

template pattern (Figure 13-10). Fold a straight edge across the top of the pattern. Slip the pattern inside the shirt neckline and place it where you want the top of the fabric insert to lie. Pin the template in place and take the shirt off.

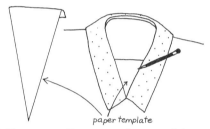

Fig. 13-10: Determine the size of the fabric insert.

10. On the template pattern, which is pinned to the shirt, trace along the inner edges of the collar. Remove the pattern and cut it along the lines you drew. Fold a piece of the insert fabric in half, wrong sides together, and pin the pattern onto the fabric with the straight edge on the fabric's fold. Mark 1″ (2.5cm) around the sides of the "v," as illustrated in Figure 13-11, and cut the insert fabric on the line of marks. Serge or zigzag stitch the raw edges of the insert.

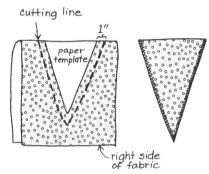

Fig. 13-11: Making the fabric insert

11. Place the fabric insert inside the neckline, pin it into place, and stitch it on. Sew on the right side of the shirt on top of the stitching that holds the bias edge in place or stitch in the ditch between the collar and the garment.

12. To complete the detail for a sailor collar, add a bow tie. Cut a piece of fabric 4½″ × 15″ (11.5cm × 38cm). Fold it in half lengthwise with right sides together. Sew along the three edges with a ¼″ (6mm) seam allowance, leaving a small opening (Figure 13-12). Clip the corners. Turn the fabric right side out and press. Sew up the opening. Tie a loose knot in the center of the fabric, and pin the center of the knot to the bottom of the collar on the front of the shirt.

Fig. 13-12: Make a bow tie for the sailor collar.

Options:

Attach the v-neck insert with Velcro so a variety of inserts could be made and worn.

Add a satin ribbon bow at the collar ends for a feminine touch.

14 Neckline Plackets

A placket worn open or closed is an attractive, comfortable neckline alteration. It relieves the feeling of close, tight-fitting ribbing and adds interesting detail to an otherwise plain neckline (Figure 14-1).

The placket can be sewn in place at the shirt's center front, on

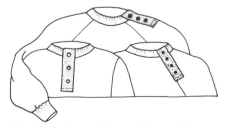

Fig. 14-1: Sweatshirt neckline plackets

the raglan sleeve seams, or on the shoulders. For each location, the sewing procedure is the same. If you feel hesitant to try this alteration on a sweatshirt, read through the directions and try the procedure on scraps of fabric to gain confidence.

Materials Needed:

- ⅓ yard (30.5cm) woven or knit fabric (Avoid thick or bulky fabrics. I prefer woven cotton fabrics and then often repeat the same fabric in part of the shirt's decoration.)
- ¼ yard (23cm) lightweight interfacing
- 3–5 buttons or other closures

1. Select the placket location and mark the vertical center line and the bottom end line with a washable marker (Figure 14-2). Measure the length and add 2″ (5cm). The pattern guide for the placket is on the next page (Pattern 14-1). The guide is only a suggested length and width and should be adjusted to your own taste. One long edge of the guide will be placed on the fold of the placket fabric. On the other long edge ¼″ (6mm) is included for the seam allowance.

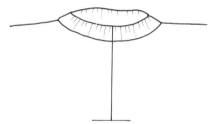

Fig. 14-2: Mark the center line and placket end on the shirt.

2. Cut two placket pieces from the fabric. Cut a piece of lightweight fusible interfacing for half of each placket (Figure 14-3). One edge of the interfacing will be on the foldline and the other edge will be on the line where the seam allowance begins. Fuse the interfacing to the wrong side of each placket piece in this position.

3. On each placket, press the seam allowances to the wrong side of the fabric. Both placket pieces should be pressed in half to *exactly* the same width. This is very important.

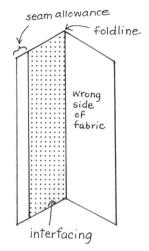

Fig. 14-3: Interfacing fused to the placket fabric

4. Place and pin one placket piece on top of the other; place them so the folded edge of one piece meets the seam allowance edge of the other piece (Figure 14-4). The top placket piece will have the folded edge to the left, seam allowance edge to the right. This is the correct alignment and opening for a placket on a woman's shirt.

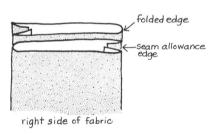

Fig. 14-4: The top placket piece has the seam allowance edge to the right.

5. With the placket pieces pinned together as described in Step #4, place the placket pieces at the bottom end line that you drew on the sweatshirt in Step #1, and pin the pieces to the shirt (Figure 14-5).

6. Sew the plackets onto the shirt with a ¼″ (6mm) seam allowance. Sew across the plackets, being careful not to sew over either edge of the placket fabrics and onto the

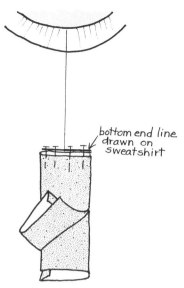

Fig. 14-5: Pin the two placket pieces to the shirt.

sweatshirt (Figure 14-6). Carefully backstitch one or two stitches on each end of the seam to make the sewing more secure, or set the stitch length to zero at each end of the seam to add extra strength.

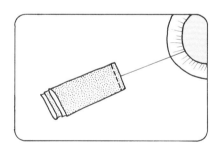

Fig. 14-6: Carefully sew the plackets to the shirt.

7. Reach for the scissors and get ready to cut the sweatshirt open so you can attach the placket sides. Proceed with confidence; you won't ruin the sweatshirt. Cut through the ribbing and the shirt front on the center line drawn on the garment. Stop 1″ above the stitching line on the plackets and very carefully cut diagonally to the exact ends of the short seam you sewed to attach the plackets to the shirt (Figure 14-7). Do not cut into the plackets themselves.

Fig. 14-7: Cut along the center placket line and then diagonally to the ends of the seam attaching the plackets to the shirt.

8. On the shirt front, bring the top placket piece up toward the neckline. Tuck the sweatshirt's cut edge about ½″ (1.3cm) inside the placket piece. (If you've chosen to attach a wide placket, cut away some of the sweatshirt fabric to avoid extra bulk inside the plackets.)

9. Pin the side of this placket piece in place. At the top, cut away some of the excess placket fabric to reduce the thickness inside the placket. Turn the raw edges of the top of the placket fabric inside the placket, folding the placket over the top of the neck ribbing (Figure 14-8). The top edge of the placket fabric should line up with the top of the neck ribbing. Pin the placket piece in place.

10. Follow the procedure in Step #9 to place and pin the other placket piece. Compare the two halves of the placket to make sure that the top edges are in line and even. Then go ahead and sew the placket sides and tops to the shirt. Sew from the right side of the sweatshirt (Figure 14-9). Stitch up from the bottom of the placket piece, along the sides and across the top.

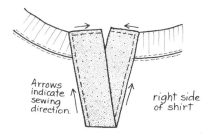

Fig. 14-9: Sew the plackets onto the sweatshirt.

11. As a final step in constructing a secure placket, reinforce the bottom of the opening. Line up the placket halves and pin in place. From the right side of the sweatshirt, sew a rectangle through both placket pieces (Figure 14-10). This stitching will permanently hold the placket sides in line and ensure a strong seam at the bottom of the opening. Now the placket opening can survive the stress of the neckline opening being stretched over someone's head.

12. Press the placket and hold it up to study it. Notice the neat bottom end of the placket and the lack

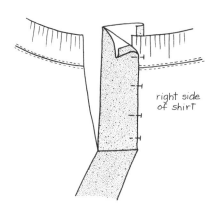

Fig. 14-8: Prepare a neat top edge for the placket.

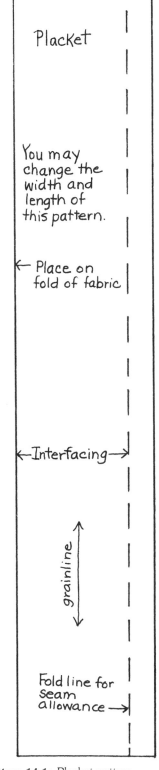

Pattern 14-1: Placket pattern

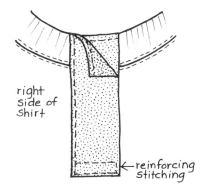

Fig. 14-10: Reinforce the placket.

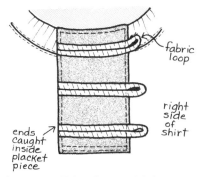

Fig. 14-11: Fabric loops added across the front of the placket

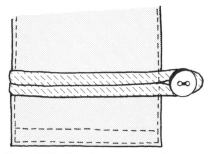

Fig. 14-12: Sew buttons onto the sweatshirt and close the placket by buttoning the fabric loops.

of wrinkles and "bloops" of fabric that often accompany placket construction. With this method, you establish a neat and straight placket end, and your sewing looks professional.

13. Do you want to add buttons and buttonholes, decorative snaps, or other closure? Now is the time to add this feature to the placket.

Options:

For one interesting closure, consider an extended fabric loop across the placket (Figure 14-11). Cut and sew long narrow tubes of fabric 2½ times wider than the placket front. Fold the tubes in half and insert the cut ends of the loops inside the top placket *before* sewing up the sides. The tube ends will be caught in the stitching that attaches the placket to the sweatshirt. Sew the loop in place on the opposite side of the top placket piece, near the edge. Sew buttons onto the sweatshirt and the loops will fit over the buttons to close the placket (Figure 14-12). You've created a button closure without the work of buttonholes! **Hint:** Before sewing large or heavy buttons onto a sweatshirt, reinforce the wrong side of the shirt with an extra piece of fabric or fusible interfacing.

You can also vary this alteration by cutting plackets wide or narrow with any variety of closures: snaps, buttons, Velcro, D-rings with ties, or ribbons. A 4″-wide (10cm) placket can be closed with one large button tied onto the shirt with a narrow ribbon sewn to the shirt (Figure 14-13). Your choices of fabrics and closures make the placket a decorative part of the shirt as well as a neckline opening.

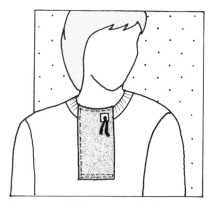

Fig. 14-13: A decorative placket

15 Ruffled Neckline

A ruffle around the neckline of a sweatshirt adds a feminine touch to the shirt. The portion of the ruffle extending onto the shirt front covers a placket opening on the raglan seam. Note that the ruffle is sewn to the top of the neck ribbing. Here's something to think about: This neckline alteration is appreciated and worn by women who like to wear turtlenecks and other necklines that stand up in the front. For other women, the ruffled addition and higher neck are uncomfortable (Figure 15-1).

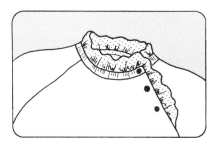

Fig. 15-1: A ruffle sewn to the top of a sweatshirt neckline

Materials Needed:

- Raglan-style sweatshirt
- ½ yard (46cm) fabric for ruffle, placket, and bias
- 3–5 buttons, approximately ½" (1.3cm) in diameter

1. Determine the length of the shirt's placket opening and place a pin to mark where the bottom of the placket will be (Figure 15-2). A 6" (15cm) opening is suggested. Be aware that a longer opening will end with the ruffle in the shirt's armpit.

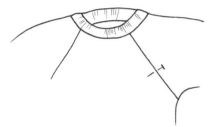

Fig. 15-2: Mark the end of the shirt's placket opening with a pin.

2. Using a tape measure on its edge, measure the length of the placket and all around the top edge of the neck ribbing. Do not stretch the ribbing. You will be adding a ruffle of this length to the placket and neckline. For a full and attractive ruffle, double the measurement to determine the length of fabric needed for the ruffle. For example, with a neck and placket measurement of 20 inches (51cm), you would cut the ruffle fabric at least 40" (101.5cm) long. I suggest the width of the ruffle fabric be 2½" (6.5cm) (finished width: 1" [2.5cm]), but you may adjust this measurement. From the same fabric as the ruffle, cut a strip of bias fabric 1" (2.5cm) wide and the length of the neckline measure only. For the placket, cut fabric 3" (7.5cm) wide and twice the length of the placket plus 2" (5cm).

3. Fold the ruffle piece in half lengthwise with wrong sides together. Press. Fold ¼" (6mm) of the raw edges of the short ends of

the ruffle fabric to the wrong side (Figure 15-3). Press. With wrong sides together, sew with a gathering stitch along the long edges of the ruffle. Gather the material and adjust the ruffles so the piece measures the length of the placket and neckline. Another idea is to pleat the ruffle fabric with small pleats.

Fig. 15-3: Fold, press, and sew the ruffle piece.

4. To staystitch the placket opening before cutting it, sew slightly less than ¼" (6mm) on each side of the raglan seam (Figure 15-4). To reinforce the end of the opening, sew back and forth across the bottom. Cut the placket open on the raglan seam between the stitching lines.

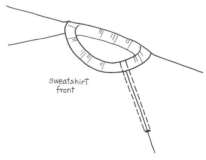

Fig. 15-4: Add staystitching and some reinforcing stitches before cutting the placket opening.

5. With the sweatshirt right side out, pin the raw edges of the gathered ruffle onto the raw edge of the placket opening, starting at the bottom of the side nearest to the shirt front (Figure 15-5). Continue pinning the ruffle around the top edge of the neck ribbing (but not down the second placket edge). Sew it onto the shirt with a ¼" (6mm) seam allowance.

6. Pin the bias strip over the raw edges of the ruffle all the way around the neck ribbing. Sew the

Fig. 15-5: Pin the gathered ruffle to the shirt neckline.

bias in place with a ¼" (6mm) seam allowance. Trim the corners of fabric, bias, and ribbing at the top edges of the neckline (Figure 15-6). The raw edges of the bias ends will be covered by the placket fabric.

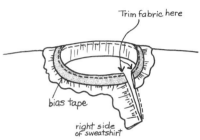

Fig. 15-6: Sew the bias strip over the ruffle on the neck edge.

7. Turn under and press ¼" (6mm) along the free edge of the bias strip. Bring the pressed edge to the wrong wide of the shirt's neckline, adjust the ruffle to stand up above the ribbing, and pin the bias strip onto the ribbing inside the neck. Hand sew the pressed bias edge into place to avoid a visible seam through the ribbing (Figure 15-7).

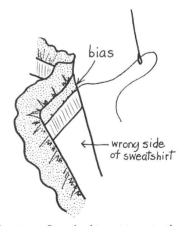

Fig. 15-7: Sew the bias strip onto the inside of the neck ribbing by hand.

8. Iron the placket fabric in half lengthwise with wrong sides together. Then fold and press the placket in half to mark the center of its length (Figure 15-8). Pin the center point at the bottom of the placket opening. Proceed to pin both halves of the placket up each side of the opening. An extra 1″ (2.5cm) of fabric will extend beyond the placket opening at the neckline edges (Figure 15-9). Sew or serge the placket onto the shirt in one continuous seam, spreading

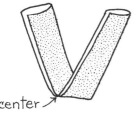

Fig. 15-8: Fold and press the placket fabric in half.

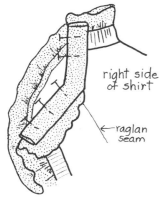

Fig. 15-9: Pin the placket band into the opening.

the opening wide when you stitch across the bottom. Use a ¼″ (6mm) seam allowance.

9. Trim the excess placket fabric and turn inside the top edges of the placket. On the side of the placket where the buttons will be sewn, plan to end the placket in line with the top of the ribbing (Figure 15-10). Press and sew or fuse the placket end closed. On the opposite end of the placket (the ruffle side), consider that a buttonhole will be sewn through the ribbing, bias end, and placket. Check the thickness of all of these layers. Cut away some of the fabrics if you think your sewing machine will be challenged by sewing a buttonhole through all the layers. As you did on the other end of the placket, trim and turn back the top edge. Sew or fuse the end on top of the

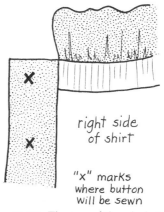

Fig. 15-10: The top of the placket is even with the top of the ribbing.

bias strip (Figure 15-11). Lean back and sigh—you're nearly done.

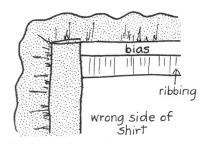

Fig. 15-11: Sew or fuse the top edge of the placket over the end of the bias on the wrong side of the sweatshirt neckline.

10. Sew buttons and buttonholes in place to close the placket opening. Buttons covered with the ruffle fabric add a nice touch. Velcro may be used to replace buttons or used in combination with buttons stitched on the shirt front.

Option:

Place the ruffle on both raglan seams of the shirt (Figure 15-12).

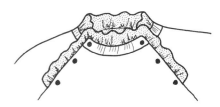

Fig. 15-12: An adaptation of the ruffle idea

16 Framed Zipper Neckline

Ready-to-wear sweatshirts with zipper front openings appeal to many sweatshirt wearers. The idea seems a great one for sewing, but the challenge of sewing a firm, woven-edge zipper to a soft, stretchable knit has discouraged many sewers. To simplify the process, try this method: Frame the zipper first with woven fabric and then sew the fabric/zipper unit to the shirt (Figure 16-1).

Fig. 16-1: Framed zipper neckline opening

Standard Framed Zipper Neckline

Materials Needed:

- ¹⁄₃ yard (30.5cm) fabric
- 7″ or 9″ (18cm or 23cm) zipper

1. Select the zipper location on the sweatshirt. The center front is a natural choice, but also look at the shoulder line or raglan seam line.

2. Cut four fabric strips for the sides of the zipper. These strips will be 2″ (5cm) longer than the zipper and 2″ (5cm) wide (or a different width, if you prefer).

3. Sandwich one side of the zipper between the right sides of two fabric strips. Match the bottom ends of the fabric strips and the zipper tape, allowing the extra fabric to extend beyond the top of the zip-

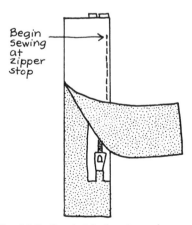

Fig. 16-2: Sandwich the zipper between two fabric strips.

per. Pin in place. Use the zipper foot and begin sewing the fabrics to the zipper at the zipper stop, leaving the strips loose at the bottom of the zipper tape. Sew close to the teeth (Figure 16-2). Press the fabric strips back, wrong sides together, exposing the zipper. Sew the other two fabric strips on the other side of the zipper, and press them back as well. At this point, the zipper will be "framed" with fabric and a back lining (Figure 16-3).

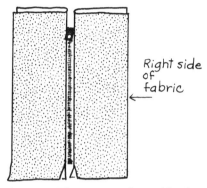

Fig. 16-3: The zipper is framed by the fabric strips.

4. On the back side of the zipper, the two fabric strips form a lining for the zipper unit. Serge finish or zigzag the long sides of both the lining strips (Figure 16-4).

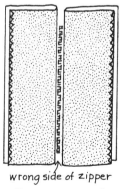

Fig. 16-4: Serge or zigzag the edges of the lining.

5. Measure across the bottom of the fabric strips and zipper to determine the width of the fabric

piece needed to finish the cloth frame. Cut one piece of fabric this width and 2″ deep for this area.

6. Before sewing this last piece of fabric to the zipper, pin the bottom ends of the lining fabric up and away from the area of the zipper stop (Figure 16-5). Place the bottom frame fabric across the bottom of the zipper unit, right sides together, and sew in place near the zipper stop (Figure 16-6). Sew this bottom piece through the front frame pieces and zipper, leaving the lining pieces loose. Remove the pins from the back lining fabric. Press the zipper and fabric frame.

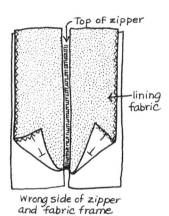

Fig. 16-5: Pin the lining strips out of the way.

Fig. 16-6: Attach the bottom frame fabric.

7. Turn under and press the raw edges of the fabric pieces surrounding the zipper front. Pin back the lining pieces to keep them out of the stitching lines when the frame unit is sewn to the shirt.

8. Position the zipper frame on the sweatshirt, wrong side of zipper against right side of sweatshirt. The top of the zipper teeth should be slightly lower than the top edge of the neck ribbing. Make sure the teeth don't extend farther (Figure 16-7). Pin the frame in place.

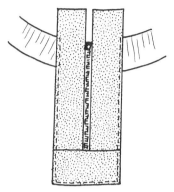

Fig. 16-7: Place the zipper frame on the front of the sweatshirt, making sure the top edge of the zipper teeth do not extend beyond the top of the ribbing.

9. Sew the zipper frame to the shirt by topstitching along the sides and bottom edges. Turn the shirt inside out and cut away the sweatshirt fabric between the stitching lines. Be careful not to cut into the zipper lining fabric. Remove the pins that held the lining strips and press the strips flat on the wrong side of the shirt.

10. Next, work with the excess fabric above the zipper and the shirt neckline. There will be plenty of excess fabric but before you cut it away, pin and plan the curve of the edges so they follow the curve of the neckline ribbing. After trimming away the extra fabric, turn each of the fabric top edges inside and sew or fuse the openings (Figure 16-8).

11. The lining strips can be attached to the shirt either by sewing or by fusing with strips or pieces of fusible web. If you decide to sew them in place, I recommend pinning them down through the right side of the shirt front. Then

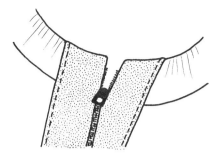

Fig. 16-8: Turn the fabric pieces inside at the top edge of the frame.

sew down each side of the front zipper frame, sewing on top of the topstitching lines.

Options:

Use decorative braid or trim instead of fabric for the sides and bottom of the zipper frame. Check your stash of trims to see the possibilities.

Use a framed zipper opening to make a cardigan opening. You'll need to buy a jacket-style zipper that opens and separates at the bottom. It should be approximately the same length as, but not longer than, the front of the sweatshirt.

Framed Zipper Neckline with Removable Fabric Facing

Materials Needed:

- ⅓ yard (30.5cm) fabric
- 7″ or 9″ (18cm or 23cm) zipper
- Velcro closures

Add a fabric facing inside the zipper opening with Velcro to create a layered look. Then the shirt can be worn with the zipper completely open to reveal a matching or coordinating fabric inside (Figure 16-9).

1. Measure the front length and width of the framed zipper. Cut a folded piece of fabric the same length as the frame and 1″ (2.5cm) wider. Serge finish or zigzag the

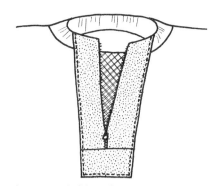

Fig. 16-9: A fabric facing inside the zipper opening

sides and bottom of the folded fabric, wrong sides together. The fold will form the top of the facing (Figure 16-10).

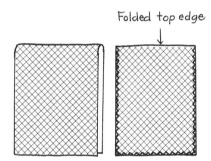

Fig. 16-10: The fabric facing

2. Place the facing inside the shirt neckline and pin it in place to determine where to sew the Velcro pieces. Narrow pieces of the fuzzy side of the Velcro will be sewn to the edges of the zipper frame lining, and the hook or rougher sides will be sewn to the facing fabric. (This is so you won't be scratched if you choose to wear the shirt without the facing.)

Option:

Even before I suggest it, you are probably thinking that several fabric facings with Velcro on the edges would be a fun way to change the look of this sweatshirt. By making the facing adjustable and removable, you will be able to change the look of the shirt and also will have no problem pulling the garment over your head.

17 "V" and Circle Necklines

By cutting a new shape for the neckline and removing the neck ribbing of a sweatshirt, a new look and comfort are added to the shirt. Circle and "v" neckline sweatshirts are difficult to find in ready-to-wear lines, but with just a few sewing steps, it's easy to create these necklines yourself. Both necklines feature a facing inside the shirt and an optional top facing can be sewn as well (Figure 17-1).

Fig. 17-1: Circle and "v" necklines

Materials Neeed:

■ ⅓ yard (30.5cm) fabric for facings

1. The first step of changing the neckline is to mark the outline of the new neck shape. For the circle neck, mark ½" (1.3cm) below the neck ribbing all around the shirt. For the "v" neckline, mark a point 2" (5cm) below the neck ribbing on the shirt's center front line (Figure 17-2). This mark will be the lowest point of the "v" neckline. (Of course, you can adjust the depth of

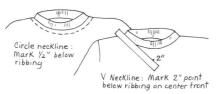

Fig. 17-2: Marking for the new circle and "v" necklines

the circle or "v" neckline, but be warned that openings even a few inches lower on the shirt front can be very revealing.)

2. For the "v" neckline, use a straightedge to draw a line from the side of the neck ribbing to the 2" (5cm) mark. Draw the line on both sides of the neckline to form the "v" shape.

3. Staystitch on the marks you drew on the shirt. For the "v" neckline, sew on the lines of the "v" and around the back of the shirt, sewing directly below the neck ribbing. For the circle neckline, sew around the neck, following the marks you drew in Step #1. Cut away the excess fabric above the staystitching, leaving slightly less than ¼" (6mm) of fabric above the staystitching.

4. Try on the shirt to test the size of the opening. If you need to, enlarge the neck opening by sewing another row of staystitching and cutting away the first row of staystitching.

5. Now that you have the outline cut for the new neckline, it's time to cut facings. Fold the sweatshirt neckline from the center front to the center back and pin. Place the folded shirt on the facing fabric, as illustrated in Figure 17-3. Note that the facing fabric is also folded.

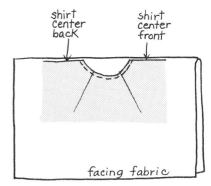

Fig. 17-3: Place the folded sweatshirt along the fold of the facing fabric.

Trace the outline of the neckline on the fabric and then remove the shirt.

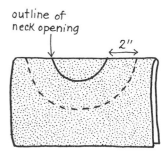

Fig. 17-4: Marking for the neckline facing

6. On the facing fabric, mark a second line 2" (5cm) from the tracing of the neck opening (Figure 17-4). Cut along both lines on the fabric to create the facing. (Borrow a detail from ready-to-wear and make the center back of the facing even wider, 5" [12.5cm]). You may wish to add lightweight interfacing to the facing. Serge or zigzag finish the outside edge of the facing (Figure 17-5). If you decide to use a second facing that would show on the right side of the sweatshirt, cut it from the same fabric as the inside facing or from a coordinating

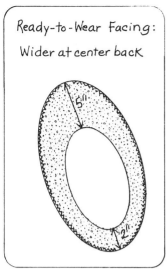

Ready-to-Wear Facing:
Wider at center back

5"

2"

Fig. 17-5: Finish the outside edge of the facing.

fabric. (I like the idea of using two different fabrics because it adds more detail to the shirt.) Instead of serging or sewing the outside edge of the second facing, turn the outside edge under about ¼" (6mm) and press.

7. It's time to sew the facings to the shirt. With the right sides together, line up the neckline edges of the sweatshirt and inside facing. Pin in place and sew the facing to the shirt with a ¼" (6mm) seam allowance (Figure 17-6). For the "v" neckline, remember that at the center front point you'll stitch one stitch across the point of the "v," as illustrated in Figure 17-7.

If you're planning to add both an inner and outer facing, place

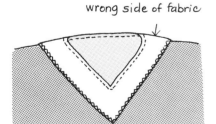

wrong side of fabric

right side of sweatshirt

Fig. 17-6: Sew the inside facing to the neckline of the shirt

Fig. 17-7: One stitch is sewn across the point of the "v."

the two facings, right sides together with the inner facing on top (Figure 17-8). Pin and sew the facings onto the shirt as described in Step #7.

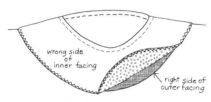

wrong side of inner facing

right side of outer facing

Fig. 17-8: The facings, right sides together with the inner facing on top

8. Trim and carefully clip the seam allowance and press the seam. For a single facing, turn the inner facing to the wrong side of the shirt and understitch (Figure 17-9). Understitching attaches the trimmed seam to the inner facing fabric, which ensures that the inner facing will stay inside the sweatshirt and not roll to the right side of the garment. Secure the inside facing to the shirt by fusing it in place with pieces of fusible web or by topstitching from the right side of the shirt.

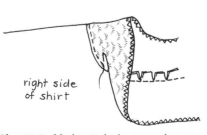

right side of shirt

Fig. 17-9: Understitch the inner facing.

9. If you are adding two facings, turn only the inside facing (the one with the serged or sewn edge) to the inside of the shirt. The outer facing is then in position for final stitching with its edge pressed back. Press and understitch the inside facing as described above. Then topstitch along the pressed edge of the outer facing from the right side of the shirt to attach both facings.

Options:

Topstitch with decorative machine stitching to add another detail to the neckline (Figure 17-10).

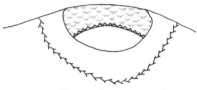

Fig. 17-10: Topstitching with a decorative stitch adds detail.

Oops! If you have accidentally created a too-deep v-neck opening, don't worry, there's a way to fix it so you can still wear the shirt. Add a fabric insert to the neckline, as described for the sailor collar (Section 13) and the framed zipper (Section 16), shown in Figure 17-11. The inserted fabric can be interchangeable and removable with the help of Velcro. (Sometimes I find that my "goofs" and sewing projects that seem to be throwaways can be salvaged; they can even turn out to be some of my favorite garments!)

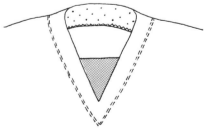

Fig. 17-11: A fabric insert in "v" neckline

18 Mock Turtleneck Made from Shirt's Bottom Ribbing

A basic crewneck sweatshirt has a 1″ (2.5cm) wide neck ribbing and a folded band of bottom ribbing of 2″ (5cm) or more. By replacing the narrow neck ribbing with a piece of the wider bottom ribbing, you change the appearance of the sweatshirt, and it gains a mock turtleneck (Figure 18-1). This change requires the use of the seam ripper to begin the process. Here's a way to use your seam ripper that is unrelated to a sewing error!

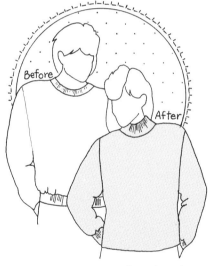

Fig. 18-1: Create a mock turtleneck.

1. Before you remove the ribbing from the neckline, staystitch around the neck directly below the ditch or topstitching that trims the neckline. Use thread that matches the sweatshirt. This stitching will maintain the size and shape of the neckline as you remove one ribbing and sew on the other (Figure 18-2).

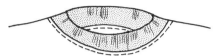

Fig. 18-2: Topstitch around the neckline.

2. Pull the neck ribbing and the shirt body in opposite directions to reveal the stitches holding the two fabrics together. Slide the seam ripper into the ditch and begin cutting the threads (Figure 18-3). This method of removing the ribbing will retain the original edge of both the ribbing and the shirt. Cut across the ribbing band so it will be a strip instead of a tube. Save the neck ribbing to use as a guide for cutting the bottom ribbing.

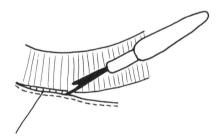

Fig. 18-3: Remove the neck ribbing.

3. Remove the shirt's bottom ribbing using the method described in Step #2. The detached ribbing is a wide folded band. Cut across the ribbing (at the seam if there is one) to make a flat strip.

4. Use the band of old neck ribbing to determine the length of the new wider ribbing for the neckline. Cut the wide ribbing to size and

unfold it. Bring the two cut edges together, right sides facing, and sew or serge to make a tube (Figure 18-4). Refold on the band's original fold, which will become the top of the turtleneck.

Fig. 18-4: The wide ribbing is ready to be added to the neck opening.

5. Mark the center front, center back, and the midpoints between on the shirt's neck opening. Mark the same quarter points on the ribbing, using the seamline as the center back. Match the marks on the ribbing and on the shirt (Figure 18-5). Pin the ribbing to the shirt,

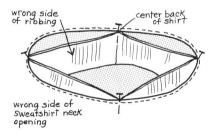

Fig. 18-5: Neck ribbing is pinned to the sweatshirt neckline. Quarter divisions of both the ribbing and the neckline are matched with the pins.

right sides together. Sew with a stretch stitch, if possible, or serge the seam around the neck with a ¼″ (6mm) seam allowance.

6. To add a final detail from ready-to-wear lines, topstitch on the right side of the neckline with a double needle. The left needle will be in the ribbing and the right needle will be in the fabric. The ditch will be centered between the needles (Figure 18-6).

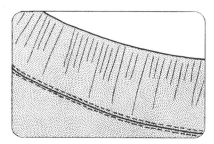

Fig. 18-6: Double-needle stitching adds detail.

7. Now you'll need to do something to the bottom edge of the sweatshirt. Simply turn up the edge of the shirt and hem it with a double needle or fashion a shirttail hemline. Check out the options in Sections 9, 20, and 21.

19 Cardigan

Opening the front of a sweatshirt to make the garment a cardigan creates a lightweight jacket and an easy-to-wear sweatshirt. Keep this alteration in mind for a person who does not want to ruin a hairdo with a pullover shirt or individuals with limited capability to lift their arms over their heads. The cardigan continues to be one of the most popular ways to alter a sweatshirt (Figure 19-1).

Fig. 19-1: Open the front of a pullover sweatshirt and turn it into a cardigan.

Materials Needed:

- ¾ yard (68.5cm) woven fabric
- ¼ yard (23cm) lightweight interfacing

- 7–9 buttons, decorative snaps, or other closures

Standard Sewn Cardigan

1. To find the center front line of the sweatshirt, create a center fold by meeting and pinning together the raglan or shoulder seams and the side seams or folds of the shirt (Figure 19-2). Mark the center front (along the fold) from the neckline to the bottom edge by pressing or marking with a washable marking pen. Remove the pins and lay the garment flat. With a yardstick and a washable marking pen, draw a clear and complete line from the top to the bottom of the shirt along the center front. It's tempting to draw just a few marks or guess at the center front line, but from experience, I've learned that taking the time to draw an accurate and complete line ensures a straight cardigan front opening.

2. Measure the length of the center line and add 2″ (5cm) to the measurement; this will be the length of the placket pattern. Use the placket pattern from Section 14 (Pattern 14-1), extending the

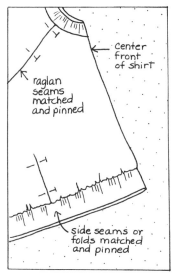

Fig. 19-2: Find and mark the true center of the shirt front by pinning the side and raglan seams of the shirt together.

pattern to the length you just calculated. Cut two long plackets from the woven fabric. Follow the notes on the placket pattern: You will place the placket guide lengthwise along the grain of fabric and on a fold. These two long strips of fabric will form the button and buttonhole bands of the cardigan front. (You may change the placket width if you wish.)

3. As noted on the placket pattern (Pattern 14-1), apply fusible lightweight interfacing to one-half of each fabric strip, from the center fold to the edge of the seam allowance line (Figure 19-3). If the fabric you've selected is soft or lightweight, you may prefer to use interfacing along the entire fabric strip between the seam allowances.

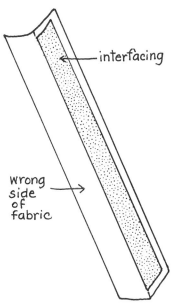

Fig. 19-3: Apply lightweight interfacing to one-half of each placket strip.

4. Now it's time to place and pin the fabric strips to the sweatshirt. With the right sides of the placket fabric facing the right side of the sweatshirt fabric, place one long edge of each strip against the shirt's center front line. The edges of the placket strips will meet at the center line. Allow 1″ of extra fabric to extend beyond both the top and bottom ends of the shirt (Figure 19-4).

5. Sew each strip to the shirt, using a ¼″ (6mm) seam allowance measured from the center front line. Sew from the bottom of the shirt to the top. These stitching lines will stabilize the knit fabric of the shirt and serve as staystitching for the shirt front opening.

6. And that's the next step—open the shirt front by cutting on the

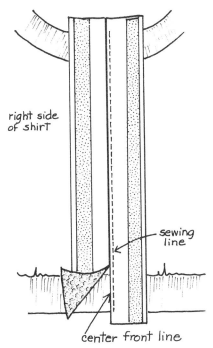

Fig. 19-4: Place the placket strips along the center front line of the shirt.

center front line between the fabric strips and stitching lines.

7. Turn the long raw edge of each strip to the wrong side of the shirt. The center fold of the strip becomes the outside edge of the cardigan opening. Press under a ¼″ (6mm) seam allowance on each raw edge, and pin each edge in place over the line of machine stitching created in Step #5. Place the pins through the shirt and placket layers from the *front* of the shirt to make it easier to remove the pins while sewing. Use plenty of pins. At the neckline and bottom edges, trim away some of the excess placket fabric to remove bulk. Turn to the inside of the shirt, and make the ends even with the neckline and bottom edges of the shirt (Figure 19-5). Pin in place.

8. To secure the fabric in place, topstitch around all edges of both fabric strips on the right side of the shirt. This will guarantee a neat and even look to the front plackets when the shirt is worn. **Hint:** To sew on and around the outside corners of the fabric strips, place a scrap of tear-away stabilizer under

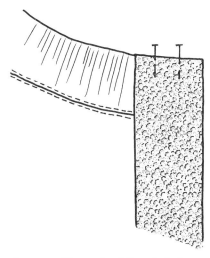

Fig. 19-5: The ends of the plackets turned inside and lined up with the top of the ribbing

the fabric. This will allow the sewing machine feed dogs to move the fabric smoothly and prevent a knot of thread from forming (Figure 19-6).

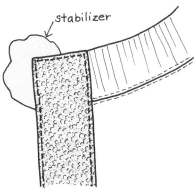

Fig. 19-6: A scrap of stabilizer placed under the outside corner of the placket

9. If you want to add closures to the cardigan, the choices include buttons and buttonholes, ties, snaps, Velcro, and any creative ideas you have.

This method of constructing a cardigan produces a neat fabric enclosure of the shirt's cut edges; no raw edges of fabric show on either side of the garment.

Speedy Serged Cardigan

Here's another way to make a cardigan sweatshirt. It involves fewer steps and takes advantage of the serger's speed and thread wrapping of raw fabric edges.

1. Find and mark with a straight-edge the shirt's center front line as described in Step #1 for the standard sewn cardigan. Staystitch along the line slightly less than ¼" (6mm) on each side. Sew from the bottom edge to the neck edge. Cut the shirt open on the center line between the stitching lines (Figure 19-7).

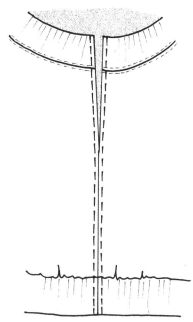

Fig. 19-7: Cut the shirt open between the lines of stitching.

2. Measure and cut the cardigan placket strips as described in Step #2 of the standard sewn cardigan. Apply fusible interfacing to the fabric if extra stability is desired.

3. Fold the placket fabric strips in half, with wrong sides together (Figure 19-8). Press.

4. On the right side of the sweatshirt, pin each folded placket strip

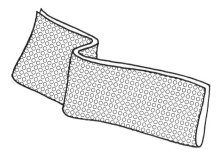

Fig. 19-8: Fold the placket bands in half.

to one of the cut edges of the sweatshirt opening, making sure the cut edges of the strip meet the cut edge of the opening. At the neckline and bottom edges, trim away some of the extra placket fabric and fold what's left to the inside of the placket so that the placket edges are even with the top and bottom ribbing (Figure 19-9).

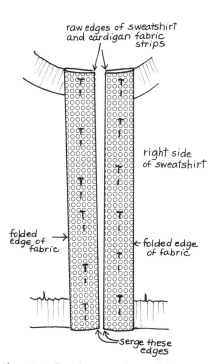

raw edges of sweatshirt and cardigan fabric strips

right side of sweatshirt

folded edge of fabric

folded edge of fabric

serge these edges

Fig. 19-9: Pin the raw edges of the bands to the raw edges of the sweatshirt front so they meet.

5. Serge stitch the placket front edges to attach the fabric strips to the shirt. Be sure to remove the pins as you serge. (Save the cutting knife edge!) Leave thread "tails" at both the beginning and end of each serged seam.

6. Press the seams toward the fabric strips. With a large-eyed hand sewing needle or a dental floss threader (Figure 19-10), thread the tails of serging back through the stitches on the garment. (It is often easier to thread the serger threads through a dental floss threader than through a needle.)

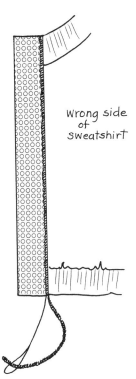

Wrong side of sweatshirt

Fig. 19-10: Thread the tails of serging through the stitching.

7. Add topstitching to the cardigan front band for extra detail.

20 Plain and Gathered Hems

On a standard sweatshirt, the bottom edge is a wide, folded band of knit ribbing. This ribbing can be detached by pulling the ribbing away from the shirt to expose the attaching threads and snipping them. Although removing the bottom ribbing shortens the shirt, it also can produce a more comfortable garment. The detached ribbing can be used to give the shirt a mock turtleneck (see Section 18). Once the ribbing is cut off, another hem must be added to prevent the bottom edge of the sweatshirt from curling. This section contains some possibilities for such hem treatments (Figure 20-1), as does Section 21.

Fig. 20-1: Sweatshirt hems without the wide ribbing

Narrow Ribbing at Bottom Edge

A narrow band of ribbing is sometimes preferred to the wide band that comes on most sweatshirts. With some cutting, folding, and sewing, you can remove the wide ribbing, cut it into a narrow band, and reattach it to the shirt's bottom edge.

First, remove the ribbing from the bottom of the sweatshirt as explained earlier in this section. If you want to use part of the detached wide band to make the mock turtleneck described in Section 18, cut off a section now. Cut the remaining piece of the detached band in half along the fold (Figure 20-2). Sew the two resulting pieces together at one set of short ends to form a long strip. Now measure the circumference of the bottom of the shirt without the ribbing. Cut the strip so it is two-thirds as long as this measurement. (Cut equal amounts of ribbing from each end of the strip so that the seams of the new ribbing band will end up at the sides of the shirt.)

Sew the short ends of the cut strip together to form a band. Fold the band in half, wrong sides together, along the long edges. Sew and band back onto the shirt with a stretch stitch or serge it, and no one will guess you have tampered with the sweatshirt.

foldline of ribbing

Fig. 20-2: Cut the wide ribbing along the fold line to make two narrower strips.

Straight Hem

The simplest hem can be created by turning the bottom edge (minus the ribbing) to the wrong side of the shirt, then pinning and sewing it in place. The edge of the sweatshirt fleece will not fray so you do not have to serge it or zigzag stitch it unless you wish to do so (Figure 20-3).

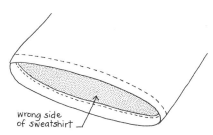

wrong side of sweatshirt

Fig. 20-3: A straight hem

When sewing the turned-up hem in place, stitch from the right side of the shirt. Use thread to match the shirt color for a neat but inconspicuous detail at the shirt's bottom edge. To borrow an idea from ready-to-wear hems, use a double needle to hem the edge (see Section 27). Experiment with stitching and loosening the top tension of the sewing machine for flatter-looking stitches. Stitching with double needles is also done from the right side of the garment (Figure 20-4).

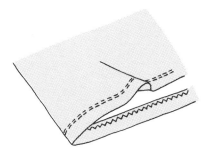

Fig. 20-4: Hem with double-needle stitching

Elasticized Bottom Edge

Materials Needed:

- Elastic

To create an elasticized bottom edge on a sweatshirt, first remove the original bottom ribbing as explained at the beginning of this section. After the ribbing is gone, turn under the bottom edge of the shirt and press it to make a 1″ (2.5cm) casing. Create a wider casing if you are using elastic wider than 1″ (2.5cm). Sew around the top of the casing, leaving a 1″ (2.5cm) horizontal opening for threading the elastic through the casing (Figure 20-5). Cut a piece of elastic to fit around the body where the sweatshirt hemline will rest. Thread the elastic through the casing. I like to use a bodkin (Figure 20-6) for this purpose. Once the elastic has been threaded, sew it into a tube by meeting the cut edges over a small pieces of fabric as shown in Figure 20-5. This method eliminates the bulk created by layers of elastic sewn together.

Drawstring Bottom Edge

Materials Needed:

- Ribbons, braid, twill tape, or cord, or fabric tubes for drawstring

To make a drawstring bottom edge, remove the sweatshirt's bottom ribbing as described at the beginning of this section. Turn under the bottom edge of the shirt and press it to make a casing wide enough to hold the drawstring you've chosen. Mark the center front at the top of the pressed-in casing, and sew a buttonhole there that is ½″ (1.3cm) to ¾″ (2cm) long (Figure 20-7). Pin the casing in place and sew around the top of the casing, above the buttonhole. Now thread the ribbon, braid, or fabric strip through the casing (Figure 20-8). Keep at least 5″ (12.5cm) of extra drawstring length on each end. These ends will form the ties that pull and gather up the shirt bottom. Tie them in a knot or bow.

Waistline Casing

Materials Needed:

- Ribbons, braid, twill tape, cord, or fabric tubes for drawstring
- ⅛ yard (11.5cm) fabric for exposed waistline casing

To give a sweatshirt some waistline definition, plan to add a casing to the waist area after hemming the bottom edge (Figure 20-9).

My favorite quick way to add a waistline casing is to sew a 1″ (2.5cm) wide strip of fabric around the outside of the shirt, leaving a small gap of ½″ (1.3cm) between the strip ends. Through the open ends I thread narrow ribbon or cording. The ends of the ribbon or tape extend 2″ (5cm) to 3″ (7.5cm) beyond the openings. When the waistline is gathered by pulling the ribbon ends, the gathering is adjusted and secured by tying the ribbon into a bow or knot. You might also think of placing the opening between the fabric ends to the side of the shirt rather than at the exact center front.

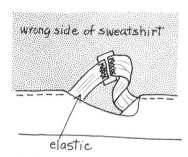

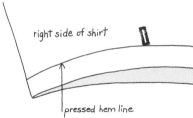

Fig. 20-7: The buttonhole is sewn directly above the hemline marking.

Fig. 20-9: A casing sewn to the waist line

Fig. 20-5: Leave an opening in the hem to thread elastic through.

Fig. 20-6: A bodkin can help thread the elastic through the hem.

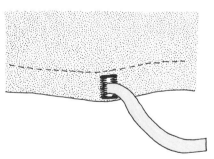

Fig. 20-8: Thread a ribbon, braid, or fabric tube through the casing.

21 Shirttail Hem

Removing the sweatshirt's bottom ribbing and adding side vents with facings makes a comfortable, nonbinding hem with more hip room. This alteration duplicates the hemline details found on ready-to-wear sportswear garments (Figure 21-1).

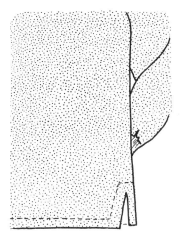

Fig. 21-1: Shirttail hemline

Materials Needed:

- ¼ yard (23cm) woven fabric
- fusible web (optional)

1. Trace the shirttail vent facing pattern from this page (Pattern 21-1) and cut two facings from fabric. The facings will not be very visible, but select fabric to complement the shirt color or the other shirt decorations. Mark the stitching and cutting lines on the wrong side of both facings. Zigzag stitch or serge the sides and top of each facing (Figure 21-2).

2. Cut the bottom ribbing off the sweatshirt. (Save it for a mock turtleneck [Section 18] or for another sweatshirt project.) A good way to remove the ribbing is to use a seam ripper to cut the threads holding

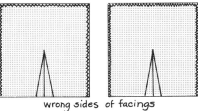

wrong sides of facings

Fig. 21-2: Sew or serge the sides and top edges of the shirttail vent facings.

the ribbing to the shirt. Once the ribbing is off the shirt, mark the exact sides of the shirt for the location of each shirttail vent with pins or a washable marker (Figure 21-3).

3. Pin the right side of each facing to the right side of the shirt, matching the marked side of the shirt with the cutting line of the facing.

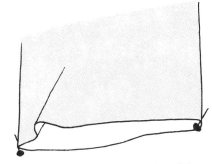

Fig. 21-3: Mark the exact sides of the shirt.

Sew on the marked stitching lines, using one stitch across the point of the "v." Cut along the cutting line carefully all the way to the point; do not cut into the stitching (Figure 21-4). Press the shirt and facing. Turn the facing to the inside of the shirt and press again.

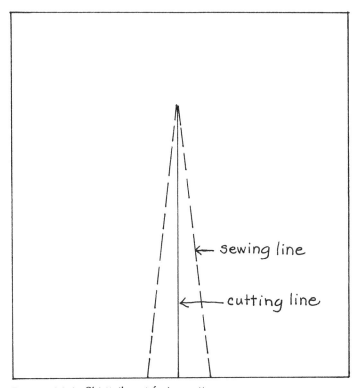

Pattern 21-1: Shirttail vent facing pattern

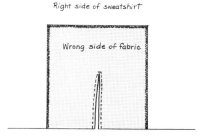

Fig. 21-4: Cut to the point of the "v."

4. A fast and invisible way to secure the facings inside the shirt is to use fusible web. Cut 1"-square (2.5cm) pieces of the web to insert under the upper corners of the facings (Figure 21-5). Fuse in place on the wrong side of the shirt. Now the facings won't show on the right side of the shirt.

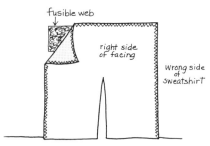

Fig. 21-5: Fusible web holds the facing to the wrong side of the shirt.

5. Next measure the length of the shirt's bottom edges between the vents. Add 2" (5cm) to each measurement and cut a 2½" wide (6.5cm) strip of fabric to sew to each half of the shirt bottom. Serge or zigzag stitch along one long edge of each strip. Place the raw edges of the fabric along the bottom edge of the sweatshirt, right sides together. Leave 1" (2.5cm) extending past the vent edge on each end of the strips (Figure 21-6).

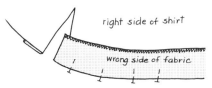

Fig. 21-6: Pin the fabric strips to the shirt's bottom edges.

6. Using a ¼" seam allowance, sew or serge the strips in place along the shirt's bottom edge. Press the seams.

7. At the vent edges, trim away some of the extra fabric of each strip. Turn the ends in to line up with the vent sides (Figure 21-7). Press each fabric strip in place on the wrong side of the shirt. Permanently attach the facings to the shirt by topstitching from the right side of the garment or by using fusible web.

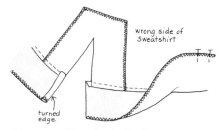

Fig. 21-7: Turn back the fabric strip end to line up with the vent edge. Pin the facing inside the sweatshirt.

Options (Figure 21-8):

Use as many shirttail vent openings as you want on the bottom hemline of the shirt.

Vary the location of the vents.

Think of using this alteration to change sleeve hems.

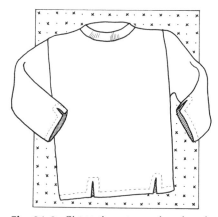

Fig. 21-8: Shirttail vents can be placed at other locations along the bottom of the shirt or on the sleeves.

22 Sleeve Changes

Sweatshirt sleeves can be altered for length, comfort, or to add detail (Figure 22-1). If the sleeves are too long or short, use any of the methods described in Section 9 for changing the sweatshirt body length. Also consider the hemline alternatives described in the Sections 20 and 21 and apply them to sleeve ends.

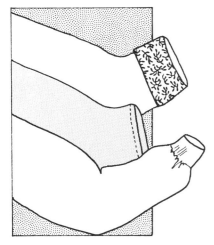

Fig. 22-1: Sweatshirt sleeve variations

Sleeves without Ribbing

If the sleeve ribbing is an undesirable finish to the sleeve ends, it can be removed. Cut away the ribbing and finish the sleeve end by turning the fabric edge to the inside of the shirt and hemming. This process will shorten the sleeve and you might prefer to cut away even more of the sleeve length to fashion a three-quarter length or short sleeve (Figure 22-2).

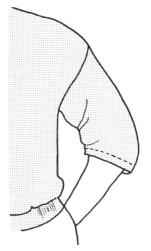

Fig. 22-2: Three-quarter length sleeve

Wide Cuffs

Wide fabric cuffs add interest to the end of sleeves from which the ribbing has been removed (Figure 22-3).

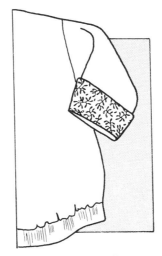

Fig. 22-3: Wide sleeve cuff

Materials Needed:

- ¼ yard (23cm) fabric for cuffs

1. After cutting away the ribbing, measure around the end of the sleeve. Add ½" (1.3cm) to the measurement for seam allowances.

2. Decide on the finished width of the cuff. I suggest 3" (7.5cm). Double the width (6" or 15cm) and add ½" (1.3cm) for seam allowances. Cut two pieces of fabric to the width and length measurements.

3. Sew each piece of fabric into a tube by sewing the 6" (15cm) edges together, with right sides facing and a ¼" (6mm) seam allowance. Press the seams. Fold each cuff in half with wrong sides together, meeting the raw edges (Figure 22-4).

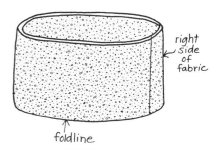

right side of fabric

foldline

Fig. 22-4: Fold the cuff tube in half.

4. Place the cuff tube in the sleeve opening and pin the raw edges to the sleeve ends, meeting the cuff and sleeve seam lines (Figure 22-5). Sew or serge the sleeve and cuff edges together, using ¼" (6mm) seam allowances. (This is one time you'll appreciate a free arm on your sewing machine.) Press the seam.

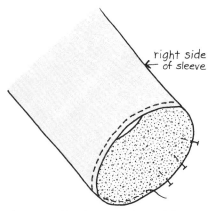

Fig. 22-5: Pin the raw edges of the sleeve and cuff together and sew.

5. Turn the cuff to the right side of the shirt (i.e., pull it out of the sleeve). Press in place and anchor

the cuff by stitching in the ditch through the cuff and sleeve seamlines (Figure 22-6).

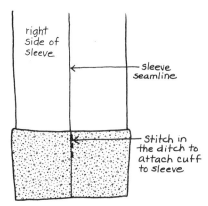

Fig. 22-6: Anchor the cuff.

Option:

For a layered-look detail, sew a second ribbing cuff inside the original sweatshirt cuff (Figure 22-7). Cut the extra cuff longer

than the original cuff so it will show underneath the original cuff. See Section 12 for instructions for sewing the cuff into the sleeve. It will look like another long-sleeved garment is being worn underneath the sweatshirt. You can fool some of the people. . . .

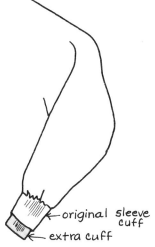

Fig. 22-7: Add a second cuff.

PART THREE
SEWING TECHNIQUES FOR TRIMMING SWEATSHIRTS

23 Machine Applique

The dictionary says that applique is the process of sewing or affixing one piece of fabric ornamentally to another piece of fabric. By using a sewing machine to do the stitching, you can add decorative applique to sweatshirts and other garments (Figure 23-1).

Machine applique is unlike many other sewing skills and requires practice, even for experienced sewers. The more time you spend practicing, the better your stitching will appear. If your applique sewing looks uneven and awkward at first, please believe that ev-

Fig. 23-1: An applique design

eryone has this experience and that your stitching will improve with practice.

Because each sewing machine operates differently, it is advisable to use the machine instruction manual to help with adjusting for applique or satin stitching. The machine applique stitch is basically a zigzag stitch packed close together so it looks more solid. The machine should be adjusted to produce wide zigzag stitches that are close together. The stitch is similar to, but wider than, the stitching on one side of a buttonhole. With practice, you will discover your own preferences for the width of the applique stitch; you might begin with a stitch width between ¹⁄₁₆″ (1.5mm) and ⅛″ (3mm). If you're just learning to applique, use a stitch with a narrow width (narrow stitches are always necessary for appliquing small designs). The narrow stitch will be easy to sew and will look neat. (Imperfections show up more clearly when a wide applique stitch is used.)

Supplies Needed

Get the best start with machine applique by assembling the correct equipment and developing good habits.

Needles. For machine applique on sweatshirts, a size 14 (90) sewing machine needle is suggested. Start with a good-quality, new needle. The needle's condition can affect the machine's performance as well as the appearance of the stitches. Expect to change needles with every major project, especially with the numerous stitches involved in any machine-applique project.

Thread. Use good-quality, new thread. (Old and inexpensive threads break easily and are inconsistent in thickness.) Begin by using all-purpose sewing threads or all-cotton threads. Make some samples and check the stitching to see if there is a difference or if one kind of thread looks better than another. After you develop your applique skills, you will enjoy using machine-embroidery and rayon threads.

For beginning applique stitching, try to match the thread color to the applique fabric. This detail will give your work a more professional look as well as blend the stitching into the fabric. For special effects (such as outlining) and as your stitching improves, use contrasting thread colors.

For most sweatshirt applique, the wrong side of applique stitching will not be seen. White thread, such as white basting thread, can be used in the bobbin. However, if there are any problems with the machine's tension, use the same thread in the bobbin as in the needle because the bobbin thread may show.

Presser foot. An open-toe presser foot is the best choice for applique stitching (Figure 23-2). Check the available presser feet for a clear plastic foot or a metal foot with an open space in the center. This space will allow you to see ahead of the stitching and guide the fabric more accurately. The presser foot will also have a groove cut in the bottom, which allows the buildup of stitching to pass smoothly under the presser foot.

Fig. 23-2: Open-toe presser foot, clear plastic or metal

Tension. (Rest easy—tension refers to the sewing machine, not your state of mind.) To produce polished applique stitching, loosen the machine's top tension slightly. Again, the machine's instruction book will tell you how to make this adjustment. You might begin with the tension setting for a buttonhole. Stitch a sample and check the stitching to see that the bobbin thread appears only on the wrong side of the stitch. Experiment with the tension setting and record the

setting that looks best in the manual or in this book.

Practicing Appliques

Now that the machine is set to go, it's time to prepare appliques for practice. A selection of practice shapes can be found within this section (Pattern 23-1). For practicing, use a piece of "background fabric" instead of a sweatshirt.

1. Trace the shapes onto paper-backed fusible web. Remember that designs with a right and left side need to be traced on the paper in a reversed position (Figure 23-3).

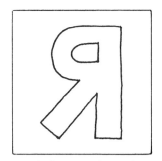

Fig. 23-3: A design with a definite right and left side must be reversed before tracing.

Use the product instruction sheet that comes with the fusible web to set the iron temperature and to fuse the paper to the wrong side of the applique fabric (Figure 23-4).

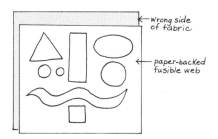

Fig. 23-4: Fusing the paper-backed fusible web (on which the designs have been traced) to the applique fabric.

2. Cut around the shapes, peel the paper off the back of the fabric, and place each design right side up

on the background fabric. Fuse the designs onto the background fabric, again following the directions provided on the product instruction sheet (Figure 23-5).

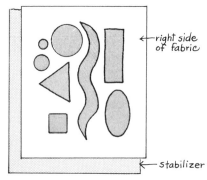

Fig. 23-5: Practice shapes are fused to the right side of the background fabric and a piece of stabilizer is placed under the fabric.

3. Now, a very important step. . . . Sound the trumpets! Before you begin to applique, add a stabilizer to the wrong side of the background fabric. Refer to the supply list in Section 2 for a list of the various types available. It is very important to place a stabilizer beneath the background fabric. A stabilizer will give a firm, stable surface for the movement of the feed dogs of the sewing machine and supports the applique stitching so it will not pucker or distort the fabrics.

At this time you are ready to begin machine applique practice. Start sewing in the center of a straight or curved edge rather than on a corner or point (Figure 23-6).

4. Posture and Attitude. Sit at the machine in a comfortable chair. Take a deep breath and rest your hands lightly on the practice fabrics. To avoid a headache and stress, concentrate on relaxing your elbows and shoulders, and you'll find that more of your body relaxes also. Begin stitching; guide the fabrics gently. Instead of stitching as slowly as possible, try "stepping on the gas" to sew a little faster. Sometimes a faster speed will make

Sweatshirt with Collar and Facings (Section 10)

I chose one fabric for the collar and another for the facings on this sweatshirt. Decorative ribbon by C.M. Offray covers the collar edges inside the neckline and is repeated on the front facing. Sewn tucks add texture to the facing fabric just above the ribbon *(see Section 9)*.

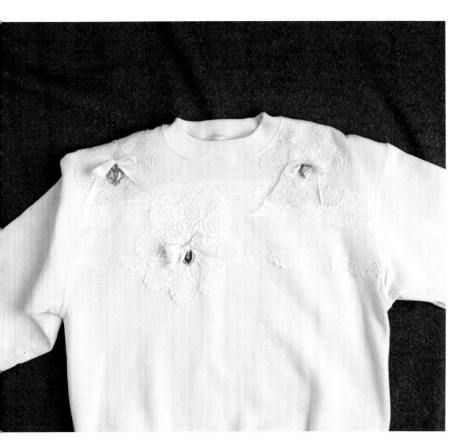

Lace-trimmed Shirt with Charms and Ribbon

For a soft, subtle trim idea, I layered lace from Liberty Fabrics and doilies on a pastel sweatshirt *(see Section 35)*. Ribbons and gold charms add extra, feminine details.

Sailor Collar Shirts *(Section 13)*

These two versions of the sailor collar include a traditional nautical style (a navy shirt with red pin-dot fabric for the trim) as well as a feminine model with lace trim and a ribbon bow.

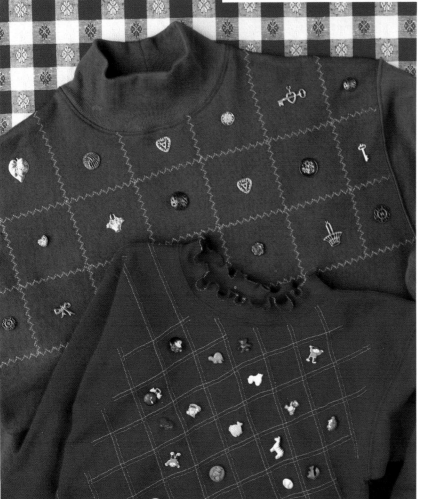

Charms and Buttons

Machine stitching and fun buttons and charms decorate these sweatshirts. The blue shirt has a turtleneck made from the shirt's original wide bottom ribbing *(see Section 18)*. The gold charms (from Creative Beginnings) and buttons on the shirt's front are outlined by gold metallic thread in a decorative stitch pattern *(see Section 28)*. Colorful children's buttons from LaMode (by B. Blumenthal) are scattered within squares formed by double-needle stitching on the red sweatshirt *(see Section 27)*. The neck ribbing of the shirt is decorated with lettuce edging *(see Section 24)*.

Nautical Trim Shirt *(Section 37)*

With a little fabric, some ribbon, and a few buttons, a navy sweatshirt takes on a nautical style. Red ribbon forms the "v" neckline that looks like a jacket opening. The shoulder epaulets (also made from ribbon) complement the shirt's nautical theme.

Postcard Applique Shirt

Several alterations and a tropical applique create this shirt's vacation theme. The original sweatshirt had a plain crew neck and wide bottom ribbing. I removed the ribbing and sewed a new hem with shirttail vents *(see Section 21)*. I then used part of the bottom ribbing to replace the shirt's original narrow neck ribbing *(see Section 18)*. The last alteration was to create a waistline by adding a casing to the right side of the shirt and inserting a decorative ribbon drawstring *(see Section 20)*. The "postcard scene" applique *(see Section 42)* was cut from cotton fabrics and Ultrasuede.

Seminole Patchwork Shirt *(Section 29)*

The technique of Seminole patchwork is combined with serger stitching to form the diagonal band of trim. To give a layered look to the sweatshirt, I added green ribbing to form a turtleneck and extra cuffs *(see Section 12).*

Three Children's Sweatshirts

Kids like stylish sweatshirts too! The bright blue shirt features a cardigan front opening *(see Section 19)* and a sailboat applique *(see Section 42).* Yarn hair trims the appliqued face on the aqua sweatshirt *(see Section 41),* and the addition of bunny ears on the hooded sweatshirt is sure to produce smiles *(see Section 36).*

Diamonds-in-a-Triangle Sweatshirt
(Section 39)

Diamond shapes cut from hand-dyed cotton (from Cherrywood Fabrics) form the triangle on this sweatshirt. The shirt also features a mock turtleneck cut from the wide bottom ribbing of the sweatshirt *(see Section 18).*

Sweatshirt with Ultrasuede Trim

This sweatshirt was sewn rather than purchased. The overlapping ribbed neckline on the shirt is part of the pattern (Stretch & Sew #387). The abstract floral design for the applique can be found in *Section 42.* Here it is rendered in Ultrasuede and highlighted with Austrian iron-on crystals from the Creative Crystal Company.

Cowls (Section 11)

Two versions of the cowl neckline are shown here. On the teal shirt, a drapey challis fabric creates the large cowl and a fabric insert coordinates with the collar's print. The cowl neckline on the black shirt features a drawstring in a casing. Reverse applique *(see Section 25)* using VIP fabric decorates the front of this shirt.

Sweatshirt with Folkwear Bib (Section 38)

Decorative ribbons and braid by C.M. Offray were sewn together to form a bib for the front of this folkwear-style sweatshirt. One of the sleeves was then decorated with additional pieces of trim.

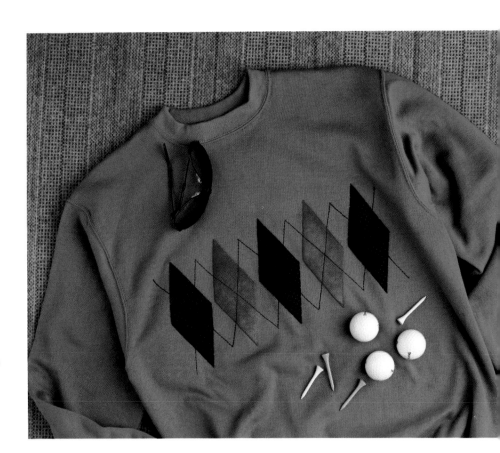

Men's Argyle Sweatshirt

The classic argyle pattern *(see Section 42)* is cut from Ultrasuede, appliqued to the shirt, and finished with decorative machine stitching *(see Section 28)*. A loop sewn into the neck band conveniently holds sunglasses or reading glasses *(see Section 41)*.

Cardigan *(Section 19)*

Elegant, gold-trimmed fabric by Hoffman California is featured in the cardigan front and argyle designs *(see Section 42)* of this stylish sweatshirt. Machine applique stitching *(see Section 23)* completes the argyle effect.

Five Sweats in a Row

Here is a whole row of sweatshirt neck-line options! At the top, eyelet lace trims the neck ribbing and raglan seam lines *(see Section 15).* On the second sweatshirt, pink lettuce edging was sewn on the center of the neck ribbing *(see Section 24).* The center shirt has a knit collar sewn to the original sweatshirt neckline *(see Section 12).* A red plack-et is added to the shoulder line of the fourth sweatshirt *(see Section 14).* Yet another placket idea is shown on the bottom shirt: a wide placket of two dif-ferent fabrics and a D-ring and ribbon closure *(see Section 14).*

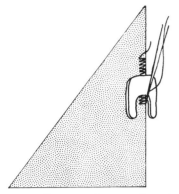

Fig. 23-6: Begin applique stitching in the center of a line.

it easier to sew smoothly around a curve or along a straight edge.

5. Pivoting. On corners, points, and small circles, you'll need to stop stitching, preferably with the needle in the fabric, raise the presser foot, and pivot the fabric. When you begin stitching again,

your first stitches might overlap some of the last stitches, and that will create a continuous line of stitching without breaks. See Figure 23-7 for examples of pivot points on various shapes. The dots indicate where the needle stops in the fabric before the fabric is turned.

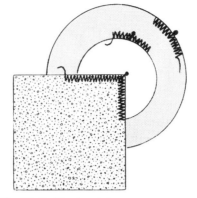

Fig. 23-7: Pivot points on a corner and on inside and outside curves

6. After stitching all the way around the pieces, overlap 2 or 3 stitches where the sewing meets the beginning stitches. Pull the top threads to the back of the fabric and knot. Tear away or remove the stabilizer. Press the design from the front and back.

Sewing the Appliques to the Shirt

Once you've practiced enough to get the feel of guiding the stitches around the applique shapes, you will be eager to trim a sweatshirt with your new sewing skill.

1. Select an applique design from Section 42 of this book or from another source. If there are many

Pattern 23-1: Practice shapes for applique

pieces or parts in the design, plan to overlap the pieces rather than abut them. Add approximately ⅛″ (3cm) to the pieces that will be placed under others (Figure 23-8).

Fig. 23-8: The leaf is cut large enough to fit under both the stem and the apple.

2. For the best placement of an applique on a garment, be sure to try the garment on and decide where the design should be sewn. This step will help you avoid design location disasters.

3. When sewing an applique onto a complete sweatshirt, you may find it awkward to have to keep other areas of the shirt out of the stitching area. Here's a hint that may help: Turn the garment inside out. You will still be sewing the applique in place on the right side of the garment, but the bulk of the garment will be above your work and is often easier to keep out of the stitching path.

4. Plan the order of stitching if pieces of the design overlap. Be sure to sew the bottom (underneath) shapes first, and begin and end sewing one or two stitches into the top shape (Figure 23-9). When you stitch around the upper

shapes, you will cover the ends of the first stitching lines.

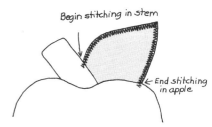

Fig. 23-9: Sew the underneath shapes first.

This is just the beginning of all the fun you will have with machine applique. Expect that you'll have to practice to build your skills and be accepting of yourself if your first efforts do not meet professional standards. Feel proud of yourself as you watch your stitching improve.

There are many fine books that provide more details about machine applique. Please refer to the bibliography for additional titles.

24 Lettuce Edging

A plain round crew neckline takes on a ruffly, feminine look with the addition of lettuce-edge stitching. The stitch used for this decoration is the applique, or satin, stitch (described in Section 23) sewn to the free edge of the ribbing (Figure 24-1).

Fig. 24-1: A ruffled edge

1. Select a thread color to match or contrast with the sweatshirt

color. Use the same thread for both the top and bobbin threads.

2. Adjust the sewing machine to the applique stitch, as described in Section 23. For a more obvious lettuce effect, use a wider setting for the stitch (a width setting of 3 or 4). Practice the stitching on a piece of ribbing or stretchy knit fabric before working on a sweatshirt.

3. Place the outside folded edge of the ribbing under the presser foot and begin sewing. As the needle swings to the left, it should stitch into the ribbing and when it moves to the right, it should stitch just over the ribbing edge (Figure 24-2).

Fig. 24-2: The lettuce-edge stitch

To create the ruffled effect, you must stretch the ribbing both behind and ahead of the needle. By holding firmly on the stretched ribbing, you will be distorting the

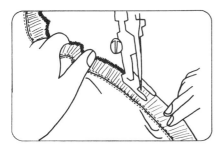

Fig. 24-3: Stretch the ribbing both behind and ahead of the needle.

edge. Adding applique stitching will prevent the ribbing from lying flat (Figure 24-3). To fill in the stitching line and make the lettuce edging look professional, sew around the ribbing twice.

4. Another way to add lettuce edging is with the serger on the rolled-hem stitch setting. By using woolly nylon thread in the serger's upper looper, you'll produce a full solid lettuce ruffle. (You'll only serge once around the neckline.) Again, plan to experiment on sample fabric before working on a sweatshirt.

Options:

Consider other locations for lettuce edging. The ends of a knit cuff can be trimmed to coordinate with the neck edge ruffle (Figure 24-4). Another possibility for ruffled edging is to place the stitch-

ing in the center of the ribbed neckband rather than at the top (Figure 24-5). Mark the center of the band all around the neckline. Pinch the ribbing at the marks, being careful to keep the back side of the ribbing out of the fold. You will stretch and sew as before but only on the front surface of the ribbing. This placement is a nice alternative for someone who finds the lettuce edging at the top of the neck ribbing to be irritating.

An interesting yoke effect is created by lettuce edging around the entire shirt body (Figure 24-6). Mark the yoke line at intervals around the shirt by measuring down from the ribbing 7″ (18cm) for an adult's shirt, 4″ (10cm) for a child's. Pin the fold around the shirt with the marks you drew falling on the crease of the fold and wrong sides together. Sew with the applique stitch on the edge of the fold, stretching the fabric behind and ahead of the sewing machine needle. Stitching around twice is recommended. You can sew additional rows of lettuce edging or vary the measurement of the yoke line to form a lower yoke in the center front and back (Figure 24-

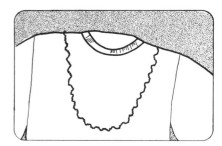

Fig. 24-7: Lettuce edging at the yoke extending down onto shirt front

7). A note of caution: Try the shirt on to plan the location of lettuce edging; avoid placing the stitching directly on the bustline.

Remember that any edge that stretches can be trimmed with the lettuce ruffle. You will notice that some ribbings and knit fabrics will stretch and ruffle more than others. Experiment with your own ideas and don't hesitate to hold the ribbing firmly to stretch the edge out of shape as you add all the stitches.

Use lettuce edging on a second layer of ribbing, which has been added to the original crewneck ribbing (Figure 24-8).

Are turtlenecks too tall and uncomfortable to wear? Try cutting

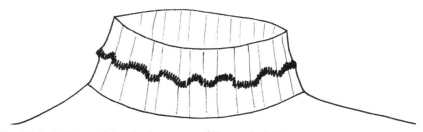

Fig. 24-5: Lettuce edging in the center of the neck ribbing

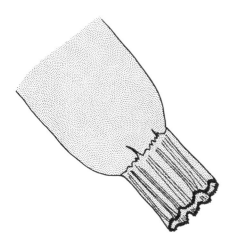

Fig. 24-4: Lettuce edging on a cuff

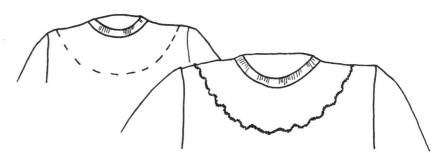

Fig. 24-6: Lettuce edging at the yoke

them down and finishing the new edge with lettuce edging, as my friend Margaret does.

Use lettuce edging as a border or frame for another decoration such as an applique or a press-on design. In Figure 24-9, the stitching begins and ends at the raglan seams of the shirt front.

Fig. 24-8: Lettuce edging trims the second layer of ribbing.

Fig. 24-9: Two rows of lettuce edging form a border for small applique designs.

25 Reverse Applique

An easy, fast way to add applique to a sweatshirt is to use the process of reverse applique. This procedure eliminates traditional applique stitching and can be done with a sewing machine that sews only straight stitches. The fabric selected for the applique shapes will be sewn to the wrong side of the garment and then the sweatshirt fabric will be cut away inside the stitching lines to reveal the fabric beneath (Figure 25-1).

Standard Reverse Applique

1. Select an applique design that has spaces between the shapes and cut fabric for each shape. Another option is to use one piece of fabric for all the shapes. The fabric pieces should be larger than the actual shapes by at least ½″ (1.3cm) all the way around. If you select cotton, rayon, or other soft fabric,

fuse lightweight interfacing to the back for additional stability and smoothness.

2. Trace the applique shapes on the right side of the sweatshirt with a washable marking pen. Carefully position and pin each applique fabric onto the wrong side of the shirt beneath the drawings of the shapes. Make sure the right side of the applique fabric is against the wrong side of the sweatshirt.

3. Sew along the lines of the designs drawn on the right side of the shirt, using a straight stitch. Use a short stitch length to make the stitching strong. Remove the pins.

4. Cut away the sweatshirt fabric from the front of the shirt to expose the applique fabric under-

Fig. 25-1: Quick-and-easy reverse applique

neath. Use sharp scissors (I prefer embroidery scissors for this type of project). Insert the scissors tip very carefully through the sweatshirt fabric and be sure to be inside the stitching lines of each shape. Cut away the shirt fabric to about ⅛" (3mm) from the stitching lines (Figure 25-2). Take your time and cut slowly. If you do cut through the applique fabric by mistake, repair a small cut by fusing another piece of interfacing onto the wrong side of the applique behind the cut.

Fig. 25-3: Decorative machine stitching added to the cut edge of the sweatshirt fabric

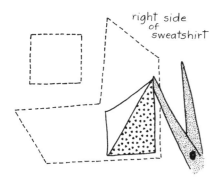

Fig. 25-2: Carefully cut through the sweatshirt fabric.

5. Although the cut edge of the sweatshirt's knit fabric will not ravel or fray, it will turn into a fuzzy edge around the designs, especially after laundering and wearing. This feature adds another detail to the design. If you prefer a flatter, sharper look, sew another row of stitching over the sweatshirt edges after cutting away the material. A decorative stitch would be a nice choice (Figure 25-3).

6. On the wrong side of the sweatshirt you may want to trim away some of the excess applique fabric. Use pinking shears and leave at least ¼" (6mm) of fabric beyond the stitching lines.

Reverse Applique with Prints and Preprinted Fabric

The same concept of reverse applique can be used with printed fabrics such as the quilt blocks of preprinted quilt-look fabrics (Figure 25-4).

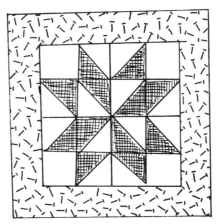

Fig. 25-4: A preprinted quilt block can be used for reverse applique projects.

1. Choose a pillow size "cheater" square for a sweatshirt front or back.

2. Pin the square to the inside of the shirt where you want the de-

sign to appear on the garment (right side of fabric to wrong side of shirt). Center the design on the garment front, or sometimes a good effect is achieved with a design that is set off-center for an asymmetrical look.

3. For this project, you will stitch the fabric to the sweatshirt by sewing from the wrong side of the garment so you can follow the pattern lines on the preprinted square.

Select portions of the quilt pattern to sew around; leave spaces between the shapes. Be sure to use a short stitch length.

4. On the right side of the shirt, cut away the sweatshirt fabric inside the stitching lines. You'll discover that the quilt square takes on a new appearance when the sweatshirt fabric shows between the design shapes.

Option:

Most preprinted pillow squares have a border design near the selvedge edges. Make use of this design by making coordinating cuffs or a collar for the sweatshirt (Figure 25-5).

Fig. 25-5: Use the coordinating fabric included with most preprinted quilt blocks to add interesting details.

26 Free Machine Embroidery

Turn your sewing machine into an artistic tool for decorating sweatshirts. With a few adjustments, you can set the machine to sew in any direction. Like a painter, you become an artist as you guide your "paint" (thread) on the fabric (Figure 26-1).

Fig. 26-1: An example of machine embroidery

Plan to spend time practicing to get the feel of maneuvering the fabric and stitching in this new way. Keep your machine's instruction book handy. It's also a good idea to treat your machine to a good dusting of the bobbin area, and oil if the manufacturer recommends that you oil the machine. Use a new size 14 (90) needle. Begin with normal tension settings and adjust them, if necessary, after practice.

1. Remove the regular presser foot and use either no foot at all, a darning spring, or a darning foot. You may find that the darning foot will hold the fabric more securely and prevent skipped stitches and broken needles (Figure 26-2).

2. Lower the feed dogs so they will not move the fabric for you as you

Fig. 26-2: Darning foot

sew. Once again, check your instruction book for how to do this. On some machines, the feed dogs are covered by a special plate; other machines have a dial or switch to raise and lower the feed dogs.

3. Set the stitch length adjustment to zero.

4. Practice on a piece of sweatshirt fabric. It's essential that the fabric be stabilized. Experiment with the variety of stabilizers available (see Section 2). The liquid stabilizer Perfect Sew has worked very well for my free machine embroidery, and the best part is that I don't have to work hard to remove the stabilizer after stitching; it simply rinses out.

5. Many free machine embroiderers use a hoop to hold the fabric while they stitch. You can experiment with this option. Make sure to add stabilizer to the fabric before applying the hoop.

6. Place the stabilized fabric under the needle, and lower the presser foot lever, even if you are not using a presser foot. (This step is easy to forget, but you will be reminded of it when you begin to sew and the machine won't work and there is

an ugly mess of thread under the fabric. Stop trying to sew, cut the threads, and begin again, with the presser foot lever down.) Hold the top thread and stitch once or twice so you can draw the bottom thread to the top of the fabric. Continue to hold onto the threads as you take the first stitches. Move the fabric yourself. Try writing your name and sewing in all directions. With practice, you will be able to guide the fabric easily and will develop a relaxed free movement for stitching (Figure 26-3).

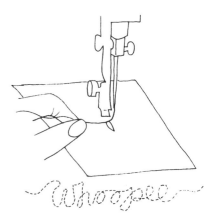
Fig. 26-3: Bring the bobbin thread to the top.

7. When you have gained the confidence to begin machine embroidering on a sweatshirt, draw a design on the shirt with a washable marker or trace an applique design. Select a thread color to match or contrast with the sweatshirt. Use the same thread in the bobbin. Before stitching, make sure to stabilize the sweatshirt fabric. If you use a liquid stabilizer, soak the area of the shirt that you plan to stitch. Hang the shirt over a heat register or fan or use a hand-held hair dryer to speed the drying process.

8. Begin stitching. As you sew around the designs, don't worry about stitching that lands off the lines. Add a second and third row of stitching, if you wish. Fill in areas of the design with a lot of stitches. Add an extra, wavy outline around the lines. The stitching will look interesting and artistic. Sew your initials or name near the design, signing your thread painting. You also can combine applique and free embroidery to create an extra dimension (Figure 26-4).

9. About the back of your sewing: Once you've completed the stitch-

Fig. 26-4: Combine an applique design and free machine embroidery.

ing, pull the threads to the back of the fabric and knot. Remove the stabilizer. You may find pin-on or press-on stabilizers easier to remove if you wet them first. Use a seam ripper or tweezers to loosen narrow or small pieces. Remove as much of the stabilizer as you can, and then leave the rest. The stabilizer remaining on the garment will soften with wear and washing and should not prove to be a problem.

This sewing and decorating technique introduces a new way to use your sewing machine. Once you get accustomed to being the pilot of the needle, you can enjoy the creative possibilities of free machine embroidery.

27 Double-Needle Stitching

For many years, a package of double needles was hiding and gathering dust in my box of sewing machine accessories. I had the needles because they came with the sewing machine, but I never considered using them (Figure 27-1).

Once I discovered that a boiled wool coat I admired had double-needle stitching as a detail, I realized that I could create the same effect with my own needles. Since

then, it's been wonderful fun to experiment and to add this detail found on expensive stylish clothing. And it's so easy to do.

A zigzag sewing machine is required if you want to sew with a double needle. The needle hole to the bobbin must be an oval rather than the small circle that a straight-stitch–only machine offers. Double needles can be purchased at a sewing machine or fabric store.

The needles are available in several sizes ranging from 1.6mm to 6.0mm. The numbers refer to the distance between the two needles. Refer to your sewing machine manual or ask a sewing machine dealer to help you determine the sizes of double needles you can use on your machine. Only the newest machines will accommodate the 6.0mm needles. Stretch double needles are also available and these needles do not skip stitches when sewing on knit fabrics.

Once the needles are installed on your machine, you're almost ready to being sewing.

1. You will need two sources of thread for the top threads, which are then drawn through all the guides to the needles. If you do not have two spools of the thread you want to use, fill a bobbin. If your machine has only one spindle, extend it by putting a drinking straw over the spindle so you can use two spools or a spool and a bobbin. One thread goes into each needle. (In case you're wondering about the bobbin, only one is needed because it services both needles. I explain this as magic.)

2. As you begin to sew, hold the two top and the bobbin threads together behind the presser foot. This gives you a good start for the stitching.

3. To produce a pin-tuck look to the parallel rows of double-needle stitching, leave the top tension at a standard setting or tighten it. For stitching that lies flatter on the fabric, loosen the top tension. Try stitching on fabric scraps before beginning a project.

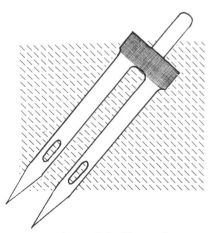

Fig. 27-1: A set of double needles

4. Use the double needles to sew any kind of a design you want. To sew a gridded design on a sweatshirt, draw two intersecting lines on the garment with a washable marker (Figure 27-2). Stitch the lines with the double needles and add more lines to form a grid by using a quilting bar as a guide to follow previous stitching lines (Figure 27-3). Add buttons, charms, or small appliques to the spaces between the grids (Figure 27-4).

Fig. 27-4: Add details between the grid lines.

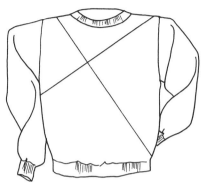

Fig. 27-2: To create a grid design start by drawing two intersecting lines on the sweatshirt.

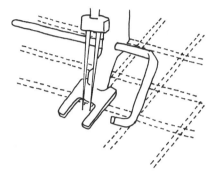

Fig. 27-3: Sew the two lines marked on the shirt and use a quilting bar to sew additional, evenly spaced lines.

You will find that double-needle stitching will not distort the size of a purchased garment but will add a quality detail and dimension to the fabric.

28 Decorative Machine Stitching

Modern sewing machines offer great collections of decorative stitches. Sometimes, the large selection of stitch possibilities is overwhelming, and making a choice from line drawings of stitches also can be difficult.

The best way to become familiar and comfortable with the decorative stitches on your sewing machine is to make a stitch sampler (Figure 28-1). Cut a piece of white or light-colored fabric large enough to sew a 1″ (2.5cm) or 2″ (5cm) line of all the decorative stitches on your machine. With a fine-line marking pen, draw lines on the fabric to make rows and sections for each stitch. Label each section with the number or code for one stitch. Use a dark thread color to stand out on the light-colored fabric and place a stabilizer under the fabric. After you've sewed all the stitches, finish off the edges of your sampler by serging, zigzag stitching, or trimming with pinking shears. Your labeled stitch sampler will serve as a handy reference at the sewing machine, and you will be able to make educated selections of decorative stitches based on the way the stitch patterns look on fabric.

Decorative stitches can be sewn directly on a sweatshirt (Figure 28-2). To ensure that the stitches lie flat and do not distort the knit fabric, be sure to place a stabilizer beneath the fabric before

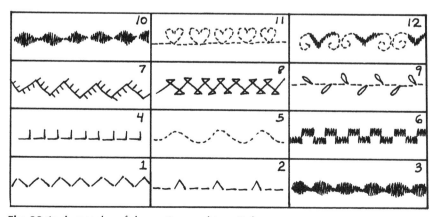

Fig. 28-1: A sampler of decorative machine stitches

56

Fig. 28-2: Decorative stitches sewn directly onto a sweatshirt

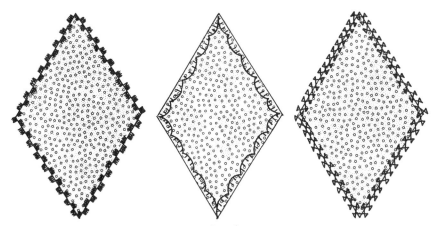

Fig. 28-3: Appliques sewn in a crazy quilt style

stitching and loosen the top tension. Use thinner embroidery, rayon, or metallic threads. I have found that stitches lie on top of the sweatshirt fleece instead of sinking into the fabric if a piece of water-soluble stabilizer is placed on top of the garment in addition to the stabilizer underneath.

Take a cue from old crazy quilts that have elaborate and elegant hand-embroidered stitches be-

tween the fabric patches (Figure 28-3). Many of these stitches, such as the feather stitch, can be duplicated on a sewing machine and added to appliques for eye-catching detail.

Many applique fabrics such as knits and Ultrasuede have non-fraying edges that do not require the heavy cover of applique stitching. Decorative stitches can be used

effectively to secure these fabrics to a sweatshirt and to complement the applique design.

Try to view all the stitch choices as an opportunity for creativity. Don't reject them just because you've never used them before. Once you begin to experiment with optional stitches, you'll enjoy the challenge of using them in many new ways.

29 Seminole Patchwork

Developed by the Seminole Indians in Florida, Seminole patchwork looks difficult and time-consuming, but it is surprisingly easy, as long as you follow the rules. Use Seminole patchwork on a sweatshirt collar or pocket or for a band of trim across the chest (Figure 29-1). The technique and measurements provided here offer only one of many ways to combine fabrics for this patchwork effect.

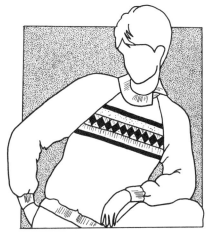

Fig. 29-1: A Seminole patchwork detail

Sewing Machine Seminole Patchwork

Materials Needed:

■ ⅛ yard (12.5cm) each of three 100% cotton fabrics

1. Begin by cutting strips of 100% cotton fabrics. Usually, the strips are cut across the grain of the fabric, from selvedge to selvedge. This will create 42″ (106.5cm) to 45″ (114cm) long strips, depending on the width of the fabric. Use three

Fig. 29-2: A strip made from three fabrics

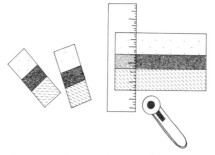

Fig. 29-4: Cutting the sewn fabrics into slices

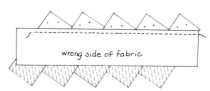

1/8″ (3mm) in from the straight edge (Figure 29-7). Trim away the jagged edges of the patchwork, and press the framing fabric over the top. Add more framing strips to increase the size of the patchwork piece.

Fig. 29-7: Sew the framing fabric to the patchwork.

fabrics to make the project strip shown in Figure 29-2. Plan the order and placement of the three fabric colors. Cut the top and bottom strips 2″ (5cm) wide. For the center strip, cut the fabric 1¼″ (3cm) wide. Note that ½″ (1.3cm) of each strip will be taken up by seam allowances (Figure 29-3). Use a rotary cutter, ruler, and mat for speedy and accurate cutting. Accurate cutting is essential for successful Seminole patchwork.

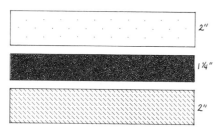

Fig. 29-3: Make three fabric strips.

2. Sew the three strips together using a ¼″ (6mm) seam allowance. Use the same seam allowance for all stitching for this patchwork project. Right sides of the fabrics will meet as you sew the long edges together. It is very important to sew carefully and to maintain an even seam allowance for all the sewing in Seminole patchwork. Press the seam allowances toward the bottom edge of the set of strips. You also can use a serger for this project. As with sewing, care and accuracy are required.

3. Next, cut the set of fabrics into slices of equal size, 1½″ (4cm) wide (Figure 29-4).

4. To create the patchwork effect, sew the slices together, right sides facing, but do not match equivalent

seam lines. As illustrated in Figure 29-5 line B on the left slice is aligned with line A on right slice. Sew or serge with right sides of the fabric together.

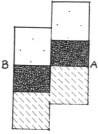

Fig. 29-5: With right sides of fabrics together, sew the slices together, lining up line B with line A of the next piece.

5. Press the seam allowances in one direction. Fuse lightweight interfacing to the back of the fabric if extra stability is desired.

6. To frame the patchwork, cut extra strips of fabric that will cover the jagged edges of the patchwork piece. Draw straight lines across the edges you plan to frame (Figure 29-6). Pin a raw edge of one of the fabric strips to the drawn line with the right sides together. Sew

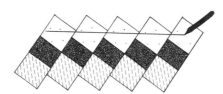

Fig. 29-6: Drawing a straight line across the edge

When you think about it, this impressive piecework is actually stripwork, because all you handle and sew are fabric strips, not squares and other small pieces. I'm always pleasantly surprised that what might seem to be tedious, repetitive work in assembling Seminole patchwork is actually fast and fun, and the result is a nice surprise.

Serger Seminole Patchwork

By using the ravel-free edge finishing capabilities of the serger, you can prepare Seminole patchwork in another way. This time, all the seam allowances will be placed on the *right* side of the fabric.

1. Cut three fabric strips in the same sizes and widths noted earlier in this section.

2. Set the serger for a three- or four-thread overlock stitch. You can use standard serger thread for the needle and loopers or a decorative thread in the upper looper. Practice serging on fabric scraps before assembling the strips for the patchwork.

3. With wrong sides facing, serge the three strips together. Also serge finish the top, bottom, and side edges of the fabrics (Figure 29-8).

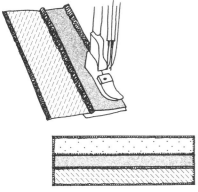

Fig. 29-8: Serge all edges and sides of the fabric strips.

4. Cut the fabric set into 1½″ (4cm) slices. Align the slices as described earlier in this section and serge the slices together. Serge with wrong sides together so the serging and seams will appear on the right side of the patchwork.

5. Place the band of serged Seminole patchwork on the diagonal on the sweatshirt front, as illustrated in Figure 29-9, or let your imagination come up with other uses and locations. To attach the patchwork to the sweatshirt, apply paper-backed fusible web to the wrong side of the fabric and then fuse the piece onto the shirt. Straight stitch

or zigzag around the edges with thread that matches or blends with the serger thread.

Fig. 29-9: Place the patchwork on the diagonal.

30 Mock Trapunto Quilting

By drawing a shape on a sweatshirt and hand or machine sewing around it, you can produce the look of trapunto quilting. The method described here offers a fast, easy way to add the detail of puffy-looking quilting without the trouble of the traditional trapunto method (Figure 30-1).

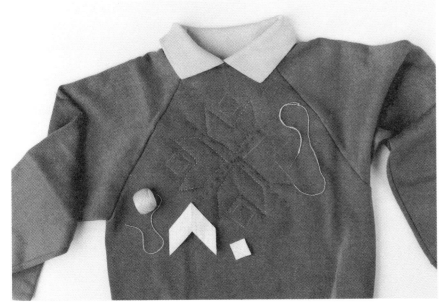

Fig. 30-1: Trapunto quilting in progress

Materials Needed:

- a piece of thin quilt batting larger than the quilting design
- thin, soft cotton or muslin fabric the same size as the batting (this fabric will not show when the garment is worn)

1. Select a quilting template or an applique design as the outline for quilting (the design shown in the figures can be found in Section 42). Cut the design from paper and trace it onto the sweatshirt with a washable marking pen or a chalk marker.

2. Cut a piece of quilt batting at least 1″ (2.5cm) larger (all the way around) than the design drawn on the shirt. Cut the cotton fabric to the same size as the batting. Pin the batting and the fabric on the wrong side of the sweatshirt underneath the design drawn on the shirt (Figure 30-2). The batting goes in between the shirt and cotton fabric.

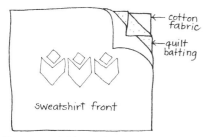

Fig. 30-2: Add one layer each of lightweight quilt batting and thin cotton fabric beneath the sweatshirt area where you will locate the quilting design.

3. The next step is basting the three layers of fabric together. (While I'd like to skip this step, I realize how necessary and important it is, so I do it carefully and suggest that you do too.) Baste by hand or machine by beginning in the center of the design and stitching through all three layers to the edge of the batting and fabric beneath. Tie knots or anchor the threads at both ends of the stitching. Stitch at least four basting lines, as illustrated in Figure 30-3. (Though I am a strong

believer in basting with thread, my sister Sarah and other friends have been successful using many safety pins instead of basting.)

4. Quilt by hand or by machine. Select a thread color to match or contrast with the shirt. With hand sewing, you could also use pearl cotton or other heavier threads to make the quilting lines more noticeable. Sew small, neat running stitches along the lines drawn on the shirt (Figure 30-4). Begin sewing at the center of the design and work your way to the edges. You will be sewing through the three layers that have been basted together. Before quilting by machine, practice sewing is advised. Baste pieces of sweatshirt fabric, batting, and cotton fabric together and experiment with stitch length, guiding the machine needle around the design lines, and holding the fabric

layers to avoid puckers in the stitching.

5. When you are ready to sew on the sweatshirt, begin sewing in the center area of the design and work toward the edges. Pull all the thread ends to the back of the garment and knot. You can also use the technique of free machine embroidery (Section 26) with this machine quilting project.

6. Remove the basting threads with care. You will notice that the design area has a puffy look caused by the batting beneath. Remove the marking lines with water or by rubbing on the chalk lines. On the back side of the stitching, trim away some of the excess batting and cotton fabric. Use pinking shears if you have them. Leave at least ½" (1.3cm) of excess fabric and batting around all the stitching lines (Figure 30-5).

Fig. 30-3: Baste through all three layers.

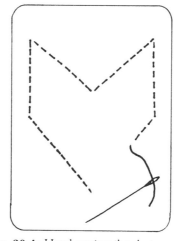

Fig. 30-4: Hand sewing the design

Fig. 30-5: Use pinking shears to cut away the excess batting and cotton fabric.

This decorating detail will give subtle dimension to the sweatshirt and is sure to be appreciated on a gift sweatshirt for a quilting friend.

31 Hand Applique

There's no doubt that sewing machines can produce many wonderful stitches and save sewing

time. However, there may be projects that you will want to do with hand-sewn applique or with fin-

ishing details you'll add with other hand sewing. (I can hear this page being turned by all of you who never want to use a hand-operated needle.)

Appliques can be hand stitched when you do not have a sewing machine nearby—for example, in the waiting room of a doctor's office and in an airplane. It usually takes no more time to finish a project by hand than by machine.

1. You will find that simple shapes are easiest to work with and sew. The applique shapes need to be cut with a ¼″ (6mm) seam allowance all the way around. Press the seam allowance to the wrong side of the fabrics after cutting. Clip into the seam allowances along curves when necessary to form the shape (Figure 31-1).

2. Pin the applique shapes to the sweatshirt. I have found that short

pins such as sequin pins work best; it is easy to use many pins if the pins are small and short. Begin pinning at the center of the shape and pin toward the edges.

3. Use a fine, small hand-sewing needle and one strand of all-purpose thread to match the applique fabric. Sew with small hidden stitches for an invisible but firm attachment (Figure 31-2).

Fig. 31-3: Hand embroidery offers detail.

Fig. 31-2: Use short sequin pins to secure the applique for hand stitching.

Options:

As a final addition, you may want to use hand embroidery to embellish the applique (Figure 31-3). Use several strands of embroidery floss, pearl cotton, or thin washable yarn.

Another idea is to sew "hobo-style" primitive stitches around the

applique (Figure 31-4). These stitches can be irregular in size and placement, deliberately imperfect.

Be careful not to pull the embroidery threads tight between the stitches. The appliques and sweatshirt should lie flat and not pucker between the stitches.

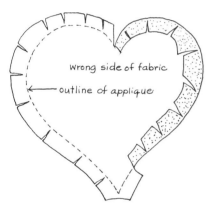

Fig. 31-1: Press the seam allowance to the wrong side of the applique design. Clipping and trimming the edges will help to produce a smooth line and accurate design shapes.

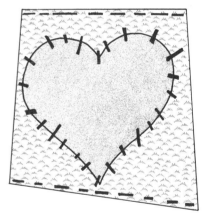

Fig. 31-4: "Hobo-style" stitches

32 Waste Canvas Embroidery

With the help of waste canvas, you can add cross-stitch embroidery to a sweatshirt. Waste canvas looks and feels like thin needlepoint canvas. It is stiff and consists

of threads woven loosely together. "Waste" refers to the threads of the canvas that are removed and discarded after the embroidery is completed (Figure 32-1).

Waste canvas is available in different sizes. The sizes, such as 10, 14, and 18, refer to the number of cross-stitches that are sewn in 1″. The cross-stitches formed

Fig. 32-1: Sweatshirt with waste canvas design and supplies

over #10 waste canvas will be larger than the those stitched over #18 canvas. I recommend sizes 14, 16, and 18 to achieve embroidery with a solid look; the individual stitches seem to blend together.

Good-quality, colorfast embroidery floss, such as DMC, is important to use. For #18 canvas use two strands (or plies) of floss, and for #14 and #16 canvas use three strands of floss. (Floss comes in six-ply skeins.) Cut the strands about 12″ (30.5cm) long. Longer threads will fray and become worn before they are worked into the design.

1. Select a charted design for the embroidery. Counted cross-stitch, knitting, and needlepoint designs can be used. Count the number of horizontal and vertical squares in the design. Count the same number of holes (spaces between threads) in the canvas to determine the amount of canvas needed for the design. Then add at least 1″ (2.5cm) on all sides for a margin around the design area.

2. The next step is very important. Position the waste canvas on the garment where you want the design to be. Make sure the canvas is straight. Baste the waste canvas onto the sweatshirt, sewing around the edges by hand or machine. The canvas must be securely attached to the garment while you are embroidering.

3. Following the charted design, cross-stitch over the canvas threads and through the sweatshirt. Knot the threads on the wrong side of the shirt fabric.

4. When the embroidery is completed, remove the basting that is holding the canvas in place. Wet the canvas so that it becomes soft and limp. Pull individual canvas threads out from under the stitching. Use tweezers to remove the canvas from areas of dense embroidery. Pull slowly and carefully on the canvas threads so you do not disturb the cross-stitching.

Removing the threads to reveal the design on the shirt is part of the fun of this handwork project. Unlike freehand cross-stitch or iron-on embroidery designs, cross-stitching over waste canvas will guarantee a very even, neat appearance to the embroidery. Consider waste canvas when you want to add a small monogram or design above a sweatshirt pocket (Figure 32-2).

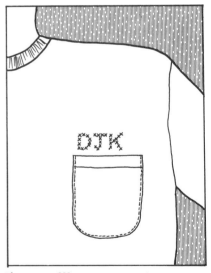

Fig. 32-2: Waste canvas embroidery

PART FOUR
SWEATSHIRT DECORATIONS

33 Pockets

A pocket on a sweatshirt can be both a useful and a decorative addition. Pocket shapes can vary from the traditional square patch-style pocket to a heart- or mitten-shaped one (Figure 33-1).

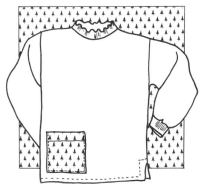

Fig. 33-2: Patch pocket

Fig. 33-1: Pockets can be decorative.

Options:

Sew a square patch pocket or two near the bottom of the sweatshirt (Figure 33-2). If the pocket will be used frequently, it is best made of two layers of fabric or one layer with fusible interfacing for stability. Pockets that are used will need help to maintain their shape and not droop. Make the pocket any size, but make sure a hand can fit inside easily. If the wearer is left-handed, make sure that the pocket is on the correct side of the shirt.

A long narrow patch pocket on the sleeve will hold pens and pencils. Place the top edge of the pocket 10″ down from the edge of the neckline or try on the shirt to ensure that the pocket will be sewn to the shirt's upper arm area above the elbow (Figure 33-3). For a right-handed individual, sew this project on the left sleeve.

Sew a zipper to fabric and build a pocket with a closure (Figure 33-4).

Cut a pocket from an old pair of jeans and sew it to a sweatshirt. (How's that for fast and easy?) Remember to sew with a size 100 or jeans needle (Figure 33-5).

A hand-warmer pocket is a large style pocket or pouch sewn to the shirt front. The sweatshirt illus-

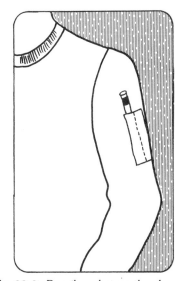

Fig. 33-3: Pencil pocket on the sleeve

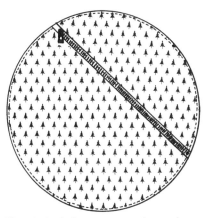

Fig. 33-4: A decorative pocket with a zipper

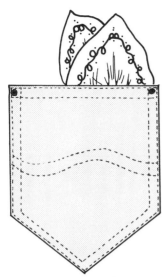

Fig. 33-5: Use a pocket from an old pair of jeans.

trated in Figure 33-6 features this type of pocket with zippers on both sides.

A more traditional style of hand-warmer pocket is patterned from a ready-to-wear sweatshirt. Make the pattern from a rectangle 8″ × 12″ (20.5cm × 30.5cm). As illustrated in Figure 33-7, trim tri-

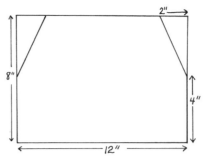

Fig. 33-7: Pattern for a hand-warmer pocket

angles off the sides of the rectangle to form the pocket openings. Cut two pattern pieces from fabric. With right sides of the fabric together, sew around the pocket shape, leaving a small opening so that you can turn the pocket right side out (Figure 33-8). Press. Sew along the pocket's top and bottom edges and partway up the sides to attach it to the shirt. Position the pocket just above the ribbing. Make sure to leave the openings so hands can be inserted (and warmed!) in the pocket (Figure 33-9).

Fig. 33-9: Sew the hand-warmer pocket to the sweatshirt.

Whether the pocket is intended for decoration or practical use, think about the fabric color and the pocket's location. If the pocket is to blend into the shirt, use a matching color. This is an important consideration for some pocket styles, especially a hand-warmer pocket located over the stomach. A contrasting color fabric will draw attention to that area of the shirt and body, which is a kind of attention many of us do not want.

The shapes and uses for pockets are numerous. When you are the sweatshirt designer, you can plan to add pockets for special needs at work or home.

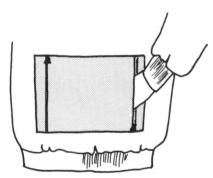

Fig. 33-6: Hand-warmer pocket with zippers

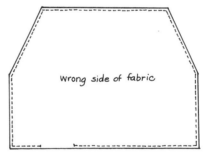

Fig. 33-8: Leave an opening in the seam for pulling out the right sides of the fabric.

34 Appliques Around the Neck

A circle of applique designs around the neckline forms attractive trim for both the front and back of a sweatshirt. For this decoration, designs are sewn onto the shirt and then the neck ribbing and part of the shirt are cut away (Figure 34-1).

Fig. 34-1: Appliques around the neckline

Solid Appliques

1. Select a design to use around the neckline. Shapes with rounded edges work best and lie flat against the body when the shirt is worn. One repeated motif (such as the heart shape shown in Figure 34-1) or a variety of shapes may be used to outline the neck edge. A heart pattern (Pattern 34-1) can be found at the end of this section.

2. Draw a circle around the neckline ¾″ (2cm) below the bottom edge of the neck ribbing (Figure 34-2). This is the line along which you will place the top edges of the appliques.

3. Measure around the new neckline and also across one of the applique shapes. Divide the neck length by the width of the applique to determine the approximate num-

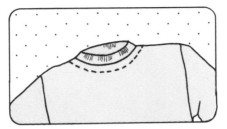

Fig. 34-2: Draw a line ¾″ below the neck ribbing.

ber of shapes needed to encircle the neck. (For example, if the neck measures 20″ [51cm] and the applique measures of 2½″ [6.5cm], divide 20″ by 2½″ to get 8. This means you will need eight appliques to encircle the neckline.) Trace the shapes onto paper-backed fusible web, fuse the web to the chosen applique fabrics, and cut out the shapes. After removing the paper backing, position the appliques on the line around the shirt's neckline. Pin the designs into place until you have arranged and adjusted them all the way around the shirt. After you are satisfied with how they are arranged, fuse the shapes onto the garment.

4. Sew around each applique with the applique stitch (Figure 34-3). See Section 23 for tips.

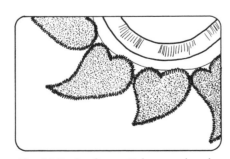

Fig. 34-3: Applique stitch around each of the designs.

5. With sharp scissors, cut around the top edge of the designs to remove the original neckline of the shirt. Do not cut through the applique stitching, and leave just a tiny bit of the shirt fabric extended beyond the applique stitching.

You might call this circle of appliques a "ring around the collar."

Cutout Applique Shapes

Instead of adding appliques, you may prefer simply to stitch with a wide applique stitch to form a scalloped neckline with eyelet cutouts (Figure 34-4).

Fig. 34-4: Scalloped neckline with eyelet cutouts

1. Draw the scallop and eyelet pattern (Pattern 34-2, found at the end of this section) around the neckline directly below the neck ribbing. Use a washable marking pen (Figure 34-5). For a different look, try drawing eyelets only in the front of the shirt or only under every other scallop.

2. On the wrong side of the shirt below the ribbing, fuse a 2″ (5cm) band of lightweight interfacing

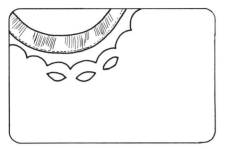

Fig. 34-5: Draw the scallop and eyelet pattern around the neckline.

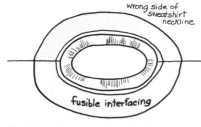

Fig. 34-6: Lightweight interfacing is fused to the wrong side of the sweatshirt neckline.

4. Attach stabilizer to the wrong side of the shirt before stitching over the scallop lines with the applique stitch. I recommend using a wide stitch setting, such as 4 or 4.5mm.

5. After sewing around the scallops and the eyelet shapes, remove the stabilizer. Use sharp scissors and trim the excess sweatshirt fabric away just above the scallop stitching line. Also carefully cut the fabric out of the eyelet shapes. Leave just a bit of fabric to avoid cutting into the stitches.

This decoration and neckline alteration will give the sweatshirt a scoop neckline with appliques or scallops framing the face and head in a flattering circle.

around the neckline (Figure 34-6). This will stabilize the shirt for sewing and wearing.

3. Stitch along the scallop line with a straight stitch. If the ribbing makes sewing awkward, cut away only the ribbing, leaving the small amount of shirt fabric above the stitching line. Pull the neckline over your head to make sure your head will fit through the opening. If it doesn't, draw and sew another row of scallops slightly below the first row and cut away the first stitching line. Try the shirt on again.

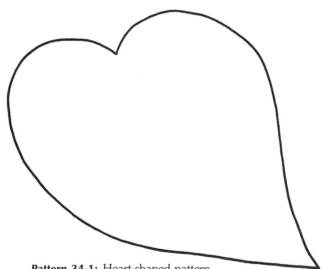

Pattern 34-1: Heart-shaped pattern

Pattern 34-2: Scallop and eyelet patterns

35 Lace Trim

Pieces of lace add unusual texture to the flat knit of a sweatshirt. Depending on the color you select for the sweatshirt, the lace details can stand out or blend into the garment. This trim suggestion offers a fast way to decorate a shirt, especially if you have a supply of lace or doilies on hand (Figure 35-1). (Make sure the lace or doilies are washable before sewing them on a sweatshirt.)

Fig. 35-1: Add lacy trim with doilies.

Options:

Find Grandma's handmade doilies that have been gathering dust in a drawer, or purchase a collection of small- to medium-size doilies. Arrange them on a sweatshirt by pinning them in place and trying the shirt on to test the locations. Once the doilies are in the right places, use several pieces of fusible web placed between the doily and the sweatshirt and spot fuse the doily onto the shirt. To protect the bottom of the iron, use a piece of the parchment paper that is left over after paper-backed

fusible web is used. Use this procedure to fuse all the doilies or lace pieces in place. Sew around the edges of each doily with either a straight or narrow zigzag stitch with thread to match the doily. Consider using small doilies as elbow patches on the sweatshirt sleeves (Figure 35-2).

A wide strip of lace can be used to form an interesting band across the front of a sweatshirt. Cut and fold the edges of the lace to meet the raglan or sleeve seams of the sweatshirt. This lace band can also be spot fused to the garment before you sew around the edges.

After sewing lace or doilies to a sweatshirt, part of the shirt beneath the lace can be cut away. Naturally, you'll want to plan the location of the cutaway areas.

Check the table linen department of stores in your area for interesting choices of laces and lace-trimmed fabrics to add to sweatshirts. Placemats, larger doilies, and

Fig. 35-2: Doilies used as elbow patches

Fig. 35-3: Dinner-roll cover

dinner-roll covers offer possibilities for more than the dining room table (Figure 35-3).

To sew a dinner-roll cover or placemat around the neckline of a sweatshirt, first remove the neck ribbing. With wrong side of fabric to right side of shirt, position the fabric trim piece on the shoulders, center front, and center back. Pin the fabric in place on the shirt. Pin around the neck hole and stitch the fabric in place around the neck by turning the shirt inside out and sewing around the top edge of the sweatshirt neck opening. Cut away the excess lace fabric, following the line of the sweatshirt neck (Figure 35-4). Test the neck opening by pulling the sweatshirt over your head. If more room is needed to get your head through, add another row of stitching ¼" (6mm) below the first row of stitching around the neck and cut away the first row. Try the fit again. Reattach the neck ribbing when the neck opening is comfortable. Pin the ribbing to the shirt, right sides together, and sew on the right side of the shirt

Fig. 35-4: Dinner-roll cover as neckline trim

around the edges of the lace fabric piece.

Would your grandmother be upset if she saw her doilies or other handwork projects on your sweatshirt? If she was an enthusiastic needlewoman, I believe she would encourage you to use her handwork in a clever new way.

36 Animal Face on a Hooded Sweatshirt

Trim the hood of a child's sweatshirt with an animal face. This decorating idea never fails to earn smiles from the child who receives the sweatshirt and from anyone who sees the hood trim (Figure 36-1).

Fig. 36-1: Animal face and ears trim the hood of a child's sweatshirt.

Materials Needed:

- paper-backed fusible web
- ⅛ yard (12.5cm) fabric for ears and nose
- 2 buttons for eyes
- yarn, cording, or pearl cotton for whiskers

Fig. 36-2: Sew two ear pieces together.

1. Using one of the ear patterns in this section, trace the outline onto paper. Cut four ear shapes from fabric. For each ear, pin two fabric shapes with right sides together and sew around the sides and top, leaving the bottom edges open (Figure 36-2).

2. Trim and press the seam. Turn the ear right side out. Turn the seam allowances of the ear bottom edges to the inside and press.

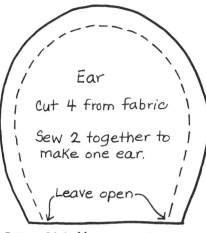

Ear

Cut 4 from fabric

Sew 2 together to make one ear.

Leave open

Pattern 36-1: Mouse ear pattern

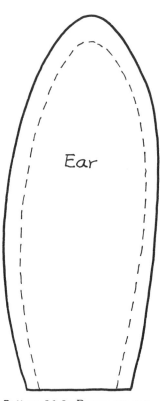

Ear

Pattern 36-2: Bunny ear pattern

3. Plan the placement of the ears, eyes, and nose. Sew the ears onto the hood by hand. (Sorry, there's just no other neat way to attach them.)

4. Trace the nose pattern onto paper-backed fusible web, and fuse the shape to the wrong side of fabric. Cut out nose, remove the paper backing, and fuse the fabric piece to the hood. Stitching details and whiskers can be added to the nose. Use yarn, thin cording, or pearl cotton for the whiskers.

5. Sew on the eyes, which can be standard buttons or the moving animal eyes available in fabric and craft shops.

This quick trim idea is fun for children to wear.

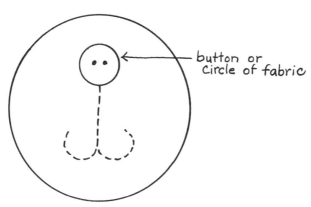

Pattern 36-3: Nose pattern

37 Nautical Trim

With ribbon, buttons, and fabric, a plain sweatshirt takes on a classic, nautical appearance (Figure 37-1). Ribbons form the look of a front opening on a double breasted jacket. (I suggest prewashing these ribbons and the other trims used.) A set-in sleeve sweatshirt with shoulder seams works best for this decorating idea. Removing the neck ribbing is required. I suggest using a navy blue sweatshirt to make the look "authentic."

Materials Needed:

- ¼ yard (23cm) white cotton fabric
- ¼ yard (23cm) lightweight fusible interfacing
- 4"-square (10cm) navy-and-white striped fabric
- 1½ yards (1.4m) of ⅜"-wide (1cm) red grosgrain ribbon
- 2 yards (1.8m) gold middy or soutache braid
- 6 gold nautical-style buttons
- 4" (10cm) red ribbing fabric for optional second neck ribbing
- 1 yard (.92m) of 1"-wide (2.5cm) navy grosgrain ribbon

- Gold metallic or clear nylon thread
- Paper-backed fusible web
- Plain fusible web
- Glue stick (optional)

1. Staystitch around the neckline before removing the shirt's neck ribbing.

2. Mark points 1" (2.5cm) from the edge of the neckline on each shoulder seam. Mark a point 8" (20.5cm) down from the center front of the shirt neckline (Figure 37-2). Using a straightedge and a white chalk marker, draw a line from each shoulder mark to the center mark. This will be the location and pattern of the white fabric "v." Make a paper pattern of this shape, extending the top edges 1"

Fig. 37-1: Nautical ribbon trim and buttons create the illusion of a jacket.

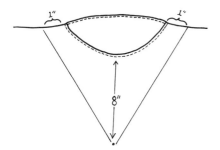

Fig. 37-2: Draw lines to connect the points.

(2.5cm) past the shoulder seams to allow leeway for final placement.

3. Most white cotton fabrics that are to be placed on a navy sweatshirt will need interfacing to prevent the dark color from showing through. Fuse interfacing to a piece of white fabric slightly larger than the "v" pattern. Next, trace the pattern on paper-backed fusible web and fuse the web to the interfaced side of the white fabric. Cut the "v" shape from the fabric.

4. Place the white fabric "v" on the sweatshirt center front and pin it in place on the shirt. Check the top ends of the fabric and trim away the excess fabric to line up the ends with the shoulder seams of the shirt (Figure 37-3). Remove the pins before fusing the white fabric "v" to the shirt body.

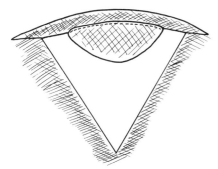

Fig. 37-3: Fusing the white fabric "v" to the shirt front.

5. Add a small triangle of the striped fabric. Use Pattern 37-1 found within this section. Note that the stripes are placed horizontally across the triangle. Trace the pat-

tern onto paper-backed fusible web, fuse to the striped fabric, cut the shape, and fuse it to the shirt center front neckline (Figure 37-4). Use navy thread and sew with the applique stitch on the sides of the triangle. Be sure to place a stabilizer beneath the shirt fabric before sewing.

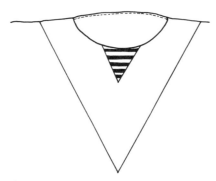

Fig. 37-4: Fuse the striped fabric triangle onto the front of the shirt.

6. Change to white thread to sew the white fabric in place on the shoulders of the shirt. Place small pieces of stabilizer under the shirt neckline at the shoulders. Applique stitch the short top edges of the white fabric along the shoulder seams (Figure 37-5). Because the long side edges of the white fabric will be covered by ribbon, it is not necessary to sew them now.

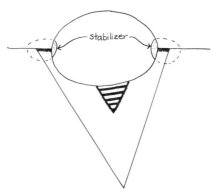

Fig. 37-5: Use white thread and applique stitching along the top edges of the white fabric.

7. You've completed all the changes and sewing at the neckline edge, so the neck ribbing can now be reattached. The shirt shown

here has a wider second ribbing of red added to the original navy one. Attach the second ribbing at this time; see Section 12 for tips.

8. The next step is to attach and sew the ³⁄₈" (1cm) red ribbon to form the look of the v-neck jacket opening. First attach the ribbon to the right side of the "v" (Figure 37-6). Cut a piece slightly longer than the side of the "v." Fold under the end that will meet the shoulder seamline. To the wrong side of the ribbon, fuse a narrow strip of paper-backed fusible web. Remove the paper and fuse the ribbon to the shirt over the edge of the white fabric.

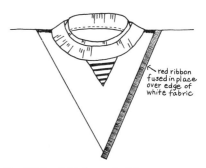

red ribbon fused in place over edge of white fabric

Fig. 37-6: Add the red ribbon.

9. On the left side of the shirt, plan out the position of the red ribbon. Fold under the end of the ribbon that will meet the shoulder seam. Extend the ribbon along the edge of the white fabric to approximately 7" (18cm) past the point of the "v." Mark this spot. At that point, fold and turn the ribbon so it is directed straight down toward the shirt bottom just above the ribbing. Cut the ribbon and measure its length. Cut a strip of paper-backed fusible web to the ribbon's length and fuse it to the wrong side of the ribbon. Fuse the ribbon in place on the shirt from the shoulder down to the point where the ribbon will be folded and turned toward the bottom of the shirt. Leave the end free temporarily.

10. Attach and sew the gold stripes before fusing the remainder of the red ribbon onto the shirt.

This way, you'll be able to cover up the ends of the gold stripes with the red ribbon. Cut three strips of gold braid, which will extend from the shoulder seam diagonally across the shirt to the line where the free end of the red ribbon will be fused in place. Place the first strip of braid approximately 2″ (5cm) below the red ribbon. Apply each of the pieces on the shirt with paper-backed fusible web or with a glue stick. Sew the strips in place with gold metallic thread or clear nylon thread (Figure 37-7).

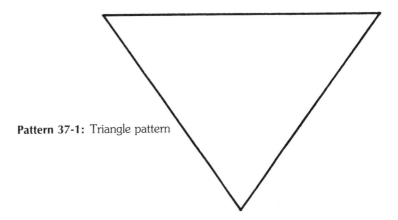

Pattern 37-1: Triangle pattern

Fig. 37-7: Plan out the locations of the red ribbon and the three gold stripes.

11. Now you can fuse the last portion of the red ribbon onto the shirt over the ends of the gold braid. Sew the long sides of both pieces of red ribbon to the shirt.

12. Finishing touches to the shirt include buttons and epaulets on the shoulders (Figure 37-8). The epaulets are made of navy and red ribbons; the navy ribbon is 1″ (2.5cm) wide and the red ribbon, ³⁄₈″ (1cm). The epaulet runs from

the edge of the sleeve seam to the edge red ribbon along the shoulder line. Measure that distance, add 1″ (2.5cm), and double the number. Cut two pieces of the navy ribbon to this length.

13. Fold the ribbon in half, wrong sides together, and fuse the two halves together with fusible web placed between the halves. Center a strip of the red ribbon over the top of the navy ribbon and fuse, wrapping and fusing the end of the

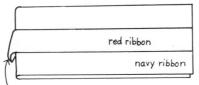

Wrap and fuse the end of red ribbon over the folded end of the navy ribbon.

Fig. 37-9: Navy and red ribbons make up the epaulet.

red ribbon over the folded edge of the navy ribbon (Figure 37-9).

14. Pin the raw edges of the epaulet on the shirt at the seamline of the sleeve, with the right side of the epaulet facing the right side of the sleeve (Figure 37-10). Sew across the shirt's seam line to attach the epaulet. Then fold the epaulet up to lie along the shoulder seam line. Sew a gold button to the free end of the epaulet to hold it in place.

15. Sew four buttons to the shirt front to complete the illusion of a jacket opening.

This decorating idea is striking in the nautical colors of navy, red, and white, but it would also work well with other color combinations such as the solid-color jewel tones featured on Amish quilts.

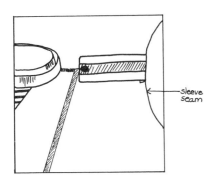

Fig. 37-8: Epaulets add to the nautical theme.

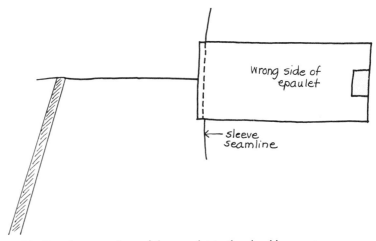

Fig. 37-10: Sew the raw edges of the epaulet to the shoulder seam.

38 Ribbons-and-Braid Folkwear Bib

With a collection of ribbons, braids, and trims, you have the makings of a sweatshirt with a folkwear look. It's a good idea to prewash all the ribbons and trims you plan to add to the sweatshirt (Figure 38-1).

Fig. 38-1: Folkwear bib created with ribbons and braid

Materials Needed:

- A variety of ribbons and braids, each at least 9″ (23cm) long
- ¼ yard (23cm) fusible interfacing
- 1⅓ yards (1.2m) bias tape or bias fabric for neck-edge trim
- 2 beads for the ends of neckline ties

1. Make the pattern for the front bib shape from two pieces of 8½″ × 11″ (21.3cm × 28cm) paper. At the top edge of each piece of paper, make a mark 2″ (5cm) from the right. At the bottom edge of each piece of paper, make a mark 4″ (10cm) from the right. Draw a line on each piece of paper to connect the two marks (Figure 38-2). The larger area to the left represents half of the bib. Cut both sheets of paper on the line and discard the smaller sections of each paper. Tape the two pattern pieces

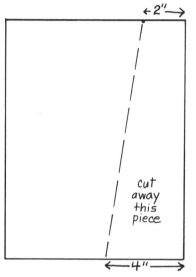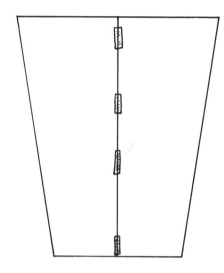

Fig. 38-2: Use two pieces of paper to create the bib pattern

together along the uncut long edge to form the entire bib pattern as shown in Figure 38-2.

2. Use the paper pattern as a guide for cutting the strips of trim. Cut all strips 1″ (2.5cm) longer than the pattern is wide. Trims and ribbons of many different colors can be combined successfully to create this bib. Experiment with a variety of colors and patterns.

3. Sew the strips together. They can be sewn to a larger piece of lightweight fabric or if you want to eliminate bulk, bring the edges of the strips together over a strip of lightweight fusible interfacing, with the fusible side facing the wrong sides of the strips (Figure 38-3). After fusing all the strips together to form the block from which the bib will be cut, zigzag stitch along the edges of the strips to secure them. Clear nylon thread works well and is invisible between the strips. Another possibility is to use thread in a contrasting color and sew with a decorative machine stitch.

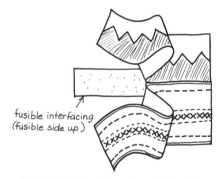

Fig. 38-3: Bring the edges of the strips together over a strip of fusible interfacing.

4. Using the paper pattern, cut out the exact shape of the bib. This will usually mean trimming away the sides of the ribbons. With additional pieces of trim, cover the raw edges of the ribbons and sew them in place (Figure 38-4).

5. Position the bib on the sweatshirt by placing the top, or wide, edge at the shoulder line and matching the center front lines of the shirt and the bib. Pin the bib

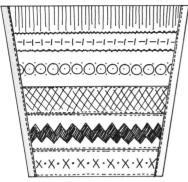

Fig. 38-4: Additional trim covers the raw edges of the bib.

into place with plenty of pins all around.

6. Staystich around the sweatshirt neckline, sewing from the wrong side of the shirt. Stitch directly below the sewing that attaches the ribbing to the garment. Cut away the neck ribbing and also the portion of the bib above the staystitching (Figure 38-5).

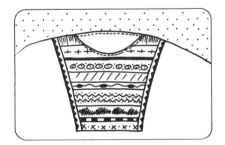

Fig. 38-5: Cut away the ribbing and bib above the staystitching.

7. Sew the outer edges of the bib to the shirt.

8. At the shirt center front, sew a line of staystitching through the shirt and bib (Figure 38-6). The stitching line can be of any length, but the shirt shown in this section has a 2″ (5cm) opening. Sew along each side of the center front line, one or two stitches from the line. Cut carefully through all layers on the center line between the stitches to form the opening in the neckline.

9. Now all that's left to do is finish the edge of the neckline. Wrap the

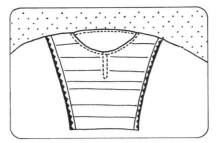

Fig. 38-6: Staystitch down the center front of the shirt.

edge with bias tape. Approximately 1⅓ yards (1.2m) of bias will be needed for the neckline and two ties. You can use packaged bias tape or cut your own. A wide bias strip works best, so plan to cut fabric bias strips at least 1¾″ (4.3cm) wide before folding and pressing in the edges (Figure 38-7). You may find it easier to wrap the bias tape around the neck edge if the shirt is trimmed close to the staystitching. Pin and sew the bias to the neckline and the front opening.

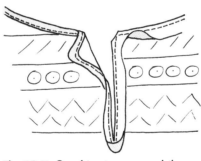

Fig. 38-7: Sew bias tape around the edge and opening of the neckline.

10. The additional bias strip can be used to make ties at the top edge of the neckline opening (Figure 38-8). Sew the ties in place after the neckline has been completed, or insert the ties in the corners of the neckline opening *before* sewing the bias strip to the neckline and opening. Slip beads onto the ties and knot the ends to hold the beads in place. Other trims also could be used for this purpose.

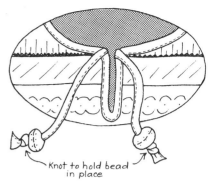

Fig. 38-8: Ties at the neckline opening

Options:

Position the ribbon strips vertically instead of horizontally.

Use fabric strips instead of ribbons and trims. Sew between them with rayon thread and decorative machine stitching.

Build the bib with Seminole patchwork strips (see Section 29).

Sew additional pieces of ribbons and trims around the sleeves. The easiest way to do this is to cut open the stitching on the lower half of the sleeve seamline so you can open the sleeve flat to sew on the trim.

Cut a facing for the back neck of the shirt (Figure 38-9). The facing is basted to the back neckline before the bias tape is attached. Cut the facing 2″ (5cm) deep at the shoulder ends and 5″ (12.5cm) deep at the center back, to duplicate back facings found in ready-to-wear lines.

Fig. 38-9: A back facing can be added.

39 Diamonds in a Triangle

Borrowing a design idea from the Texas star quilt, the diamonds in a triangle are sewn together and centered on the front of the sweatshirt or off-set for an asymmetrical look (Figure 39-1). The triangle is most easily placed on the shirt if the neck ribbing is removed and later reattached or replaced with another neck treatment.

Fig. 39-1: A quilting accent

Materials Needed:

■ 6 fabrics, ⅛ yard (11.5cm) to ¼ yard (23cm) each

1. After selecting the six fabrics for this design, decide on the order of placement. Fabric #1 will be the single diamond placed the bottom of the triangle. Fabric #2 will be the second row of two diamonds, and so forth, with six diamonds of fabric #6 at the top, or neck, edge (see Figure 39-2).

2. Use the diamond template found on this page (Pattern 39-1) to cut the 21 diamond shapes needed to form the triangle. Note the grain line direction on the pat-

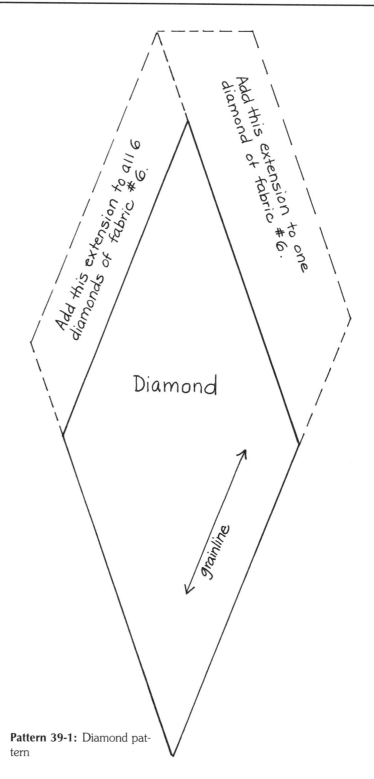

Add this extension to all 6 diamonds of fabric #6.

Add this extension to one diamond of fabric #6.

Diamond

grainline

Pattern 39-1: Diamond pattern

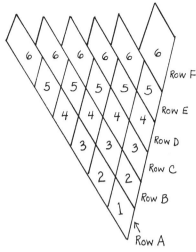

Fig. 39-2: Placement of six fabric colors in rows

tern. The fabric #6 diamonds can be cut with the same diamond pattern, but you may want to increase the size of these diamonds so that more of the fabric will show on the shirt. To do this, add the extension on the left side of the diamond shape for five of the diamonds, and for the sixth diamond, add both the left extension and the right extension.

3. Arrange the diamond shapes on a flat surface to form the triangle. Place the largest fabric #6 diamond in the far right position of the layout (see Figure 39-2). Collect the diamonds by rows to sew or serge together. Use a ¼″ (6mm)

seam allowance. Row A will have one diamond of each fabric. Row B will have diamonds of fabrics #2–#6. Sew all the rows. Then sew or serge all six rows together to form the triangle.

4. Lay the triangle on the sweatshirt to decide on the placement. Pin the entire fabric piece onto the shirt.

5. Staystitch around the neck from the wrong side of the garment. Sew next to the stitching that attaches the neck ribbing to the shirt. Remove the shirt's neck ribbing and also trim the triangle fabric that extends above the staystitching line (Figure 39-3).

6. The next step is to sew the sides and top edges of the triangle to the shirt. The raw edges can be

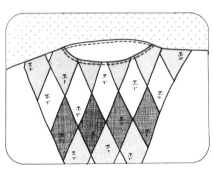

Fig. 39-3: Remove the ribbing and trim the triangle fabric that extends above the staystitching line.

pressed under and topstitched to complete the trim or extra bands of fabric can be sewn over the raw edges. Use another fabric, bias tape, or ribbon trim to cover the raw edges of the triangle (Figure 39-4).

7. After the triangle shape is completely sewn in place, it's time to reattach the neck ribbing. On the shirt illustrated in Figure 39-1, I replaced the narrow neck ribbing with a wider piece from shirt's bottom ribbing. The remaining wide ribbing was then cut in half, sewn into a narrow band of ribbing, and reattached to the bottom of the shirt.

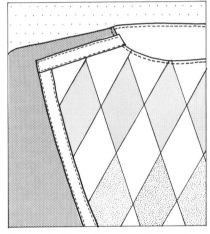

Fig. 39-4: Cover the raw edges of the triangle.

40 Stenciling and Painting Designs

Stenciling is an early American decorating technique revived for both home decor and fabric detail. Use stencils and fabric paint to add a designer touch to sweatshirts.

Look for special fabric paints at sewing and craft stores. Once applied and dried on fabric, the paints last through laundering and wear. It is best to read and follow

the paint manufacturer's directions for applying the paints and to practice on other fabric before decorating a sweatshirt.

You can use a pre-cut stencil

or make your own. To make a stencil, draw or trace a design onto firm paper, such as a file folder. (One design possibility is shown in Pattern 40-1 at the end of this section.) Use a razor blade or sharp scissors to carefully cut the design out of the paper. Cut from the middle of the design and work outward.

Take a piece of cardboard larger than the area to be stenciled and place it inside the sweatshirt (Figure 40-1). The cardboard will prevent the paint from soaking through to the back of the shirt. Tape the stencil to the front of the shirt and apply paint to the area within the designs. Many expert stencilers prefer to use only a small amount of paint on a brush, but you should experiment on your own to decide how to handle the brush and paint. Slight imperfections add to the charm of stenciling

and not every design shape is expected to look exactly like the one next to it. (That's what appeals to me about stenciling—perfection is not expected.)

To further embellish stenciling after the paint dries, add decorative sewing stitches (see Section 28) or free machine embroidery (see Section 26) to build a dimensional look to the artwork. This idea is for those of you who won't be satisfied with just painting but have to sew too (Figure 40-2).

Fabric paints in narrow tip squeeze bottles can be used to apply a thin line of paint to outline an applique in place of applique stitching (Figure 40-3). Before outlining with paint, you may want to secure the edges by fusing the appliques to the sweatshirt with paper-backed fusible web and then sewing around the shapes with a narrow zigzag stitch.

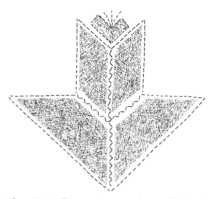

Fig. 40-2: Decorative stitches add detail to a stenciled design.

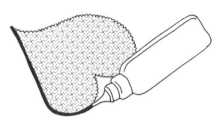

Fig. 40-3: Paint used to seal the edge of an applique

Fine, small details on appliques are easy to add with paint. Eyes and other facial features can be quickly painted on animal or human faces. These details can be stitched on, but painting is faster.

Fabric paints can also be applied with household sponges or potatoes cut into design shapes. Once again, experimentation is the key to success.

You are certain to discover great potential for fabric painting as you experiment. For additional details and instruction in painting, read *Fabric Painting Made Easy,* by Nancy Ward (Chilton, 1993).

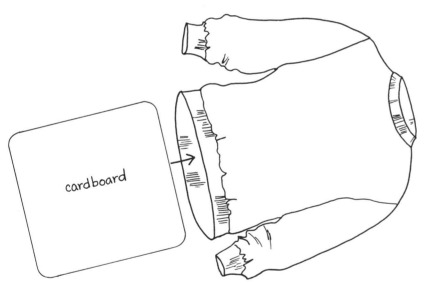

cardboard

Fig. 40-1: Cardboard prevents the paint from soaking through to the back of the sweatshirt.

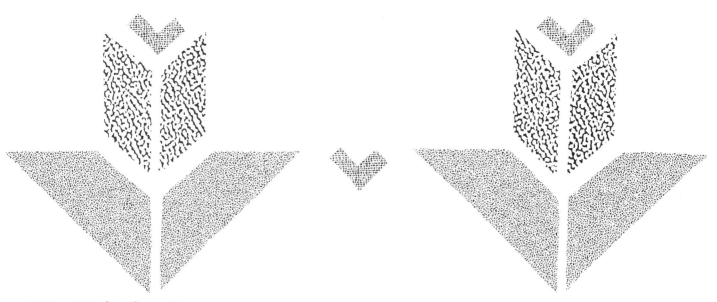

Pattern 40-1: Stenciling pattern

41 A Collection of Trims and Details

Here are more ideas for embellishment and special details to attend to before your sweatshirt creation leaves the sewing room.

Look closely at the buttons in your collection. Pick out some interesting or unusual ones to add to a sweatshirt; it's a great way to showcase part of your collection or a grouping of new buttons fresh from the fabric store. Small buttons also make good substitutes for eyes on appliqued faces and add dimensional interest to the center of a flower (Figure 41-1).

Add sparkle to a sweatshirt with sequins or Austrian crystals. If you don't see yourself as a sequin kind of person, add just a few sparkles to highlight a design.

Attach yarn hair around an appliqued face and mirror the face of the special little girl wearing the shirt. If the girl's hair is curly and short, wrap washable yarn around a strip of paper 1½" (4cm) wide and 8" (20.5cm) long. Machine sew

through the center of the strip with thread that matches the yarn (Figure 41-2). Tear away the paper. The yarn loops will twist and turn and become a row of curls you can sew around a face.

For the little girl who wears braids, cut twelve pieces of yarn 14" (35.5cm) long. Divide the yarn into three bunches and braid them. Tie ribbon bows to the end of the

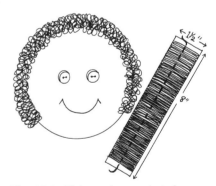

Fig. 41-2: Make curly yarn hair for an appliqued girl's face.

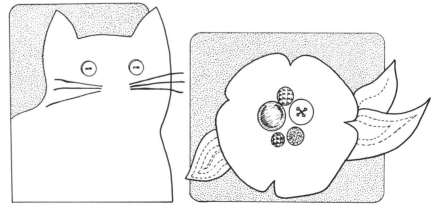

Fig. 41-1: Button details on a face and flower

braided strip. Hand sew the braid around the 3″ (7.5cm) circle face (Figure 41-3).

Fig. 41-3: Braid washable yarn for hair and tie with ribbons.

Plastic squeakers beneath appliques increase the appeal with their musical feature (Figure 41-4). Squeakers are popular with children and make fun surprises for adults.

Here's how to attach a squeaker properly. Begin by cutting a 3″ (7.5cm) square of applique fabric. Put the squeaker on the sweatshirt where the applique will

Fig. 41-4: Squeaker

be placed. The fabric square is placed over the squeaker and the edges pinned down. With the zipper foot on the sewing machine, sew closely around the squeaker using a straight stitch (Figure 41-5). This procedure will hold the squeaker in place beneath the applique. Trim away the excess fabric close to the stitching line.

Select an applique larger than the squeaker. Put the applique piece on top of the fabric covering the squeaker. Hold the applique in place over the squeaker by using a glue stick. Applique the design in place. The squeaker will survive machine washing and drying at moderate temperatures.

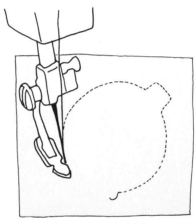

Fig. 41-5: Sew a piece of fabric over the squeaker.

Sew a loop of fabric into the ditch between the neck ribbing and sweatshirt front (Figure 41-6). This loop will be especially easy to add if the neckline of the shirt is altered and the neck ribbing is removed.

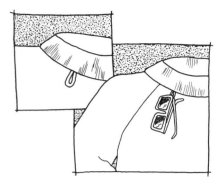

Fig. 41-6: A loop for glasses

The loop holds a pair of reading or sunglasses. A fabric tube or strip 1½″ (4cm) long provides enough material when folded in half to allow for a seam allowance and to hold a pair of glasses.

The final addition to any sweatshirt you decorate is a label with the artist's (your) name (Figure 41-7). Order labels printed with your name or make your own labels with a fabric marker or the alphabet and lettering system on your sewing machine. Consider yourself a sewing artist with many talents and abilities. It's only right that you sign your work as other artists sign theirs.

Fig. 41-7: A personalized label

42 Finding Applique Designs and Inspiration

Collecting applique designs becomes a hobby once you become excited about the applique technique. The pages that follow offer a variety of designs to begin your collection. Many other applique patterns and books are available as well.

Before applique pattern books were widely available, children's coloring books were used for design shapes. A review of current coloring books will quickly reveal the problem of very detailed drawings, which are a challenge to the applique process. The best choices in coloring books are the ones for the youngest children, basic ABC shapes and simple designs.

You will want to expand your design collection to include more adult or sophisticated and contemporary designs.

Look around you. Notice patterns in draperies and carpeting.

Look at gift wrap, greeting cards, and company logos on billboards. Study shapes in nature. Consider your cookie cutter collection and the motif repeated on the paper towels in your kitchen. Do "research shopping" in department stores to study current design themes in ready-to-wear lines.

Gift and clothing catalogs offer an abundant supply of applique ideas. Cut out the pictures of appliqued clothing and other items. Glue the photos, their descriptions, and prices into a notebook to look at when you need ideas for a special project. Note the simplicity of the design shapes and the kinds of fabrics used to create the appliques. Also notice the prices and remind yourself that as an applique artist, you have a valuable sewing skill.

Make notes and drawings of applique ideas you find. Add them to your notebook or put them in a file folder or (one of my favorite collection sites) a shoebox. Even if your drawing skills are minimal, make sketches of the designs you see. Buy a tablet of tracing paper. This sheer paper will make it easy to trace designs for your inspirational collection. The enlarging capability of a copy machine may help you to turn your drawings into full-size applique patterns. Always save at least one copy of the original full-size patterns you make. It's frustrating to cut up the only copy you have and later to wonder how it all fits together.

It's an enjoyable challenge to keep your eyes open to applique design possibilities. Use your notes and picture collections to plan a personal designer touch for a sweatshirt, and when the shirt is done, take a picture to record your work.

Quilt Blocks

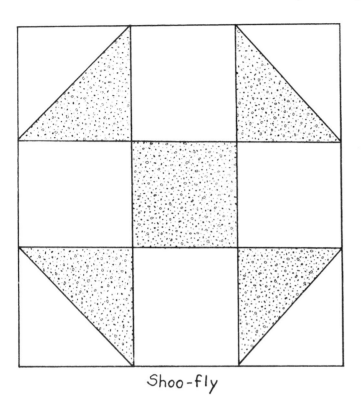

Shoo-fly

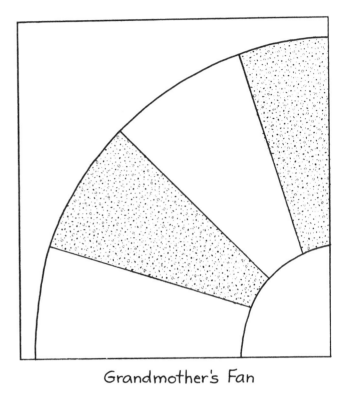

Grandmother's Fan

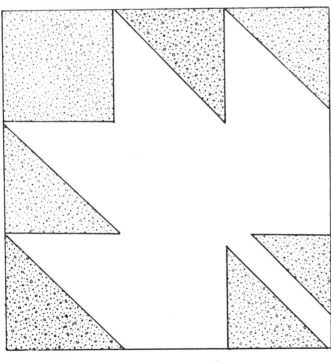

Maple Leaf

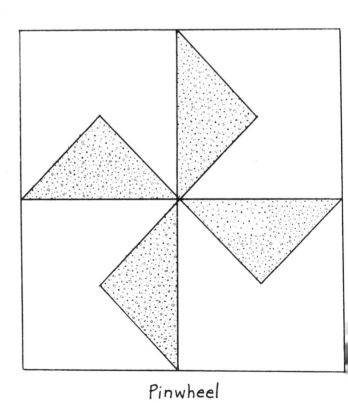

Pinwheel

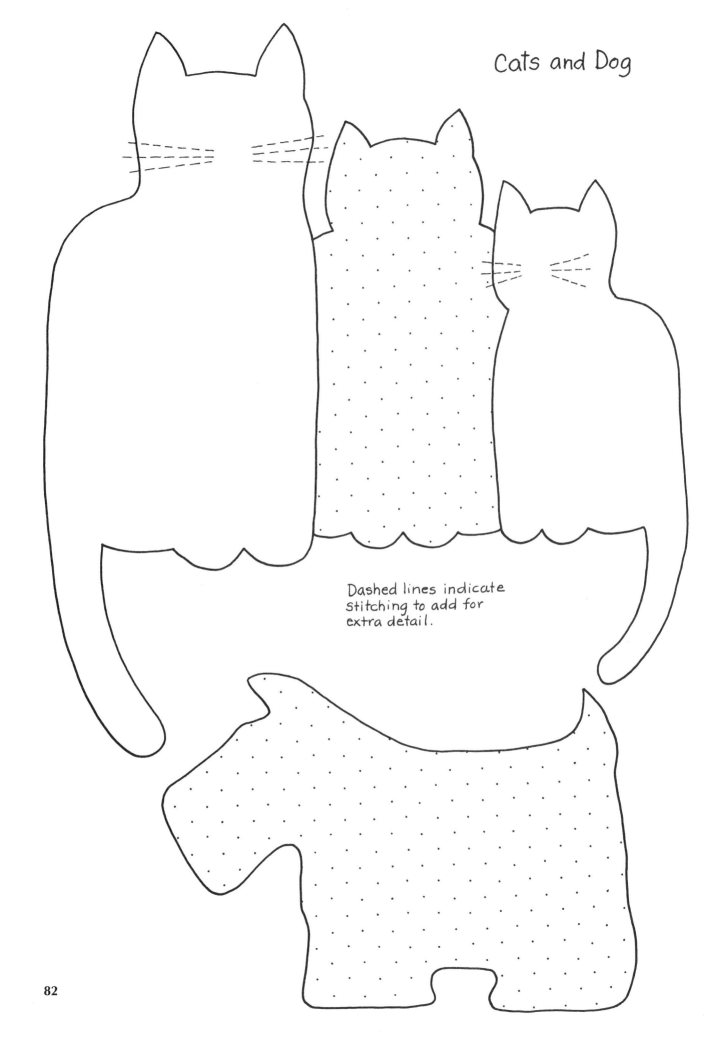

Cats and Dog

Dashed lines indicate
stitching to add for
extra detail.

Scandinavian Designs

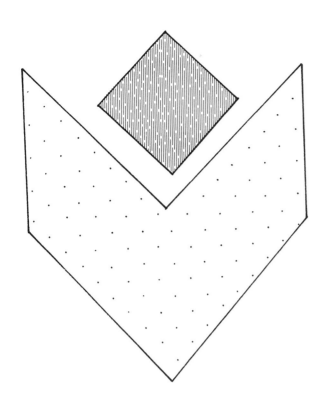

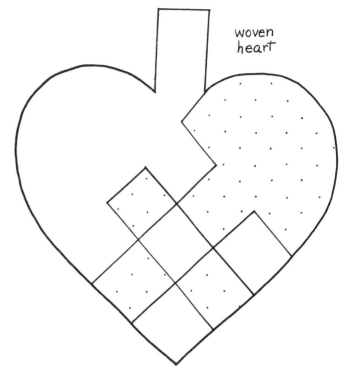

woven heart

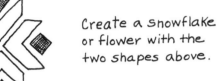

Create a snowflake or flower with the two shapes above.

Scandinavian elves

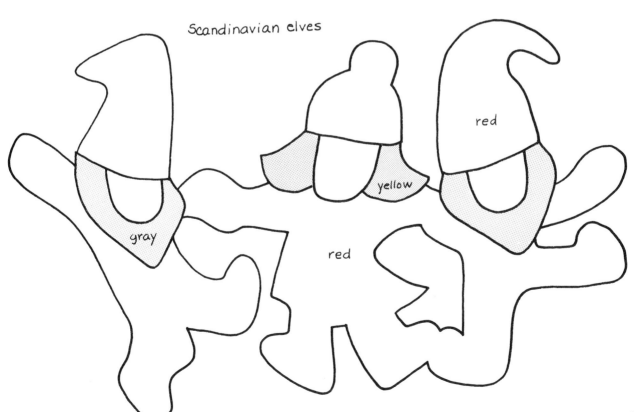

gray

yellow

red

red

green

yellow

red

blue

brown

white   white

white

Make this "postcard" scene by
stitching the palm tree, sun,
and sailboat over a 6½" x 4½"
rectangle of blue fabric.

red

white

red

fishing
bobber

Clown Innovations:

Substitute buttons for the fabric circles the clown is juggling.

Use small pieces of washable yarn for the clown's hair.

A ribbon with a knot in the center can become the clown's bowtie.

Houndstooth

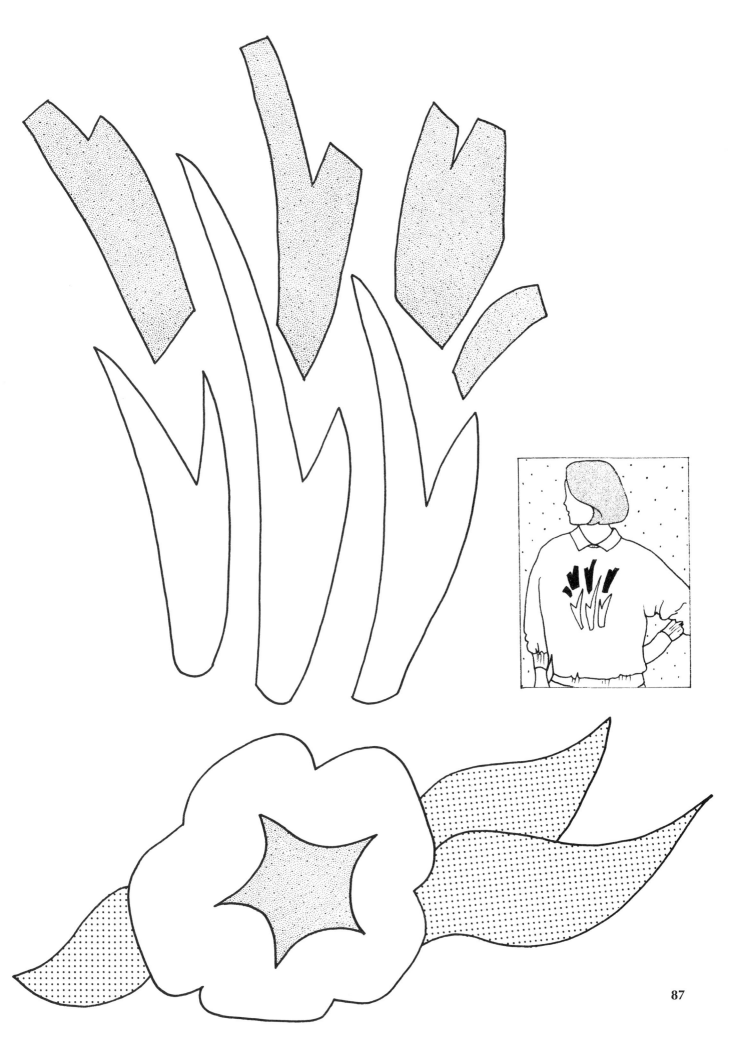

Hearts

88

Birds

Dashed lines indicate stitching detail.

Skater's Sweatshirt

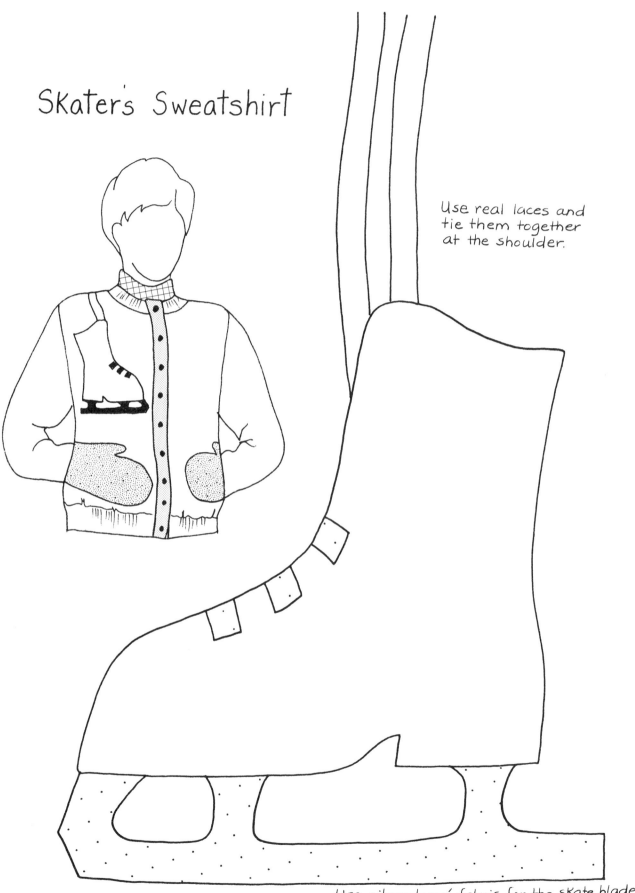

Use real laces and tie them together at the shoulder.

Use silver lame' fabric for the skate blade

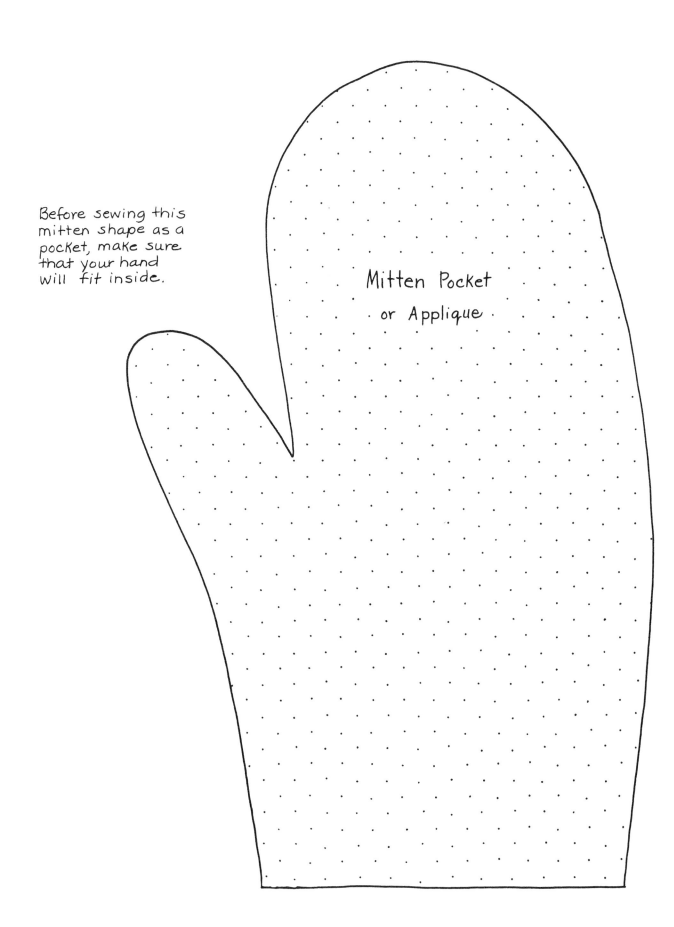

Before sewing this mitten shape as a pocket, make sure that your hand will fit inside.

Mitten Pocket

or Applique

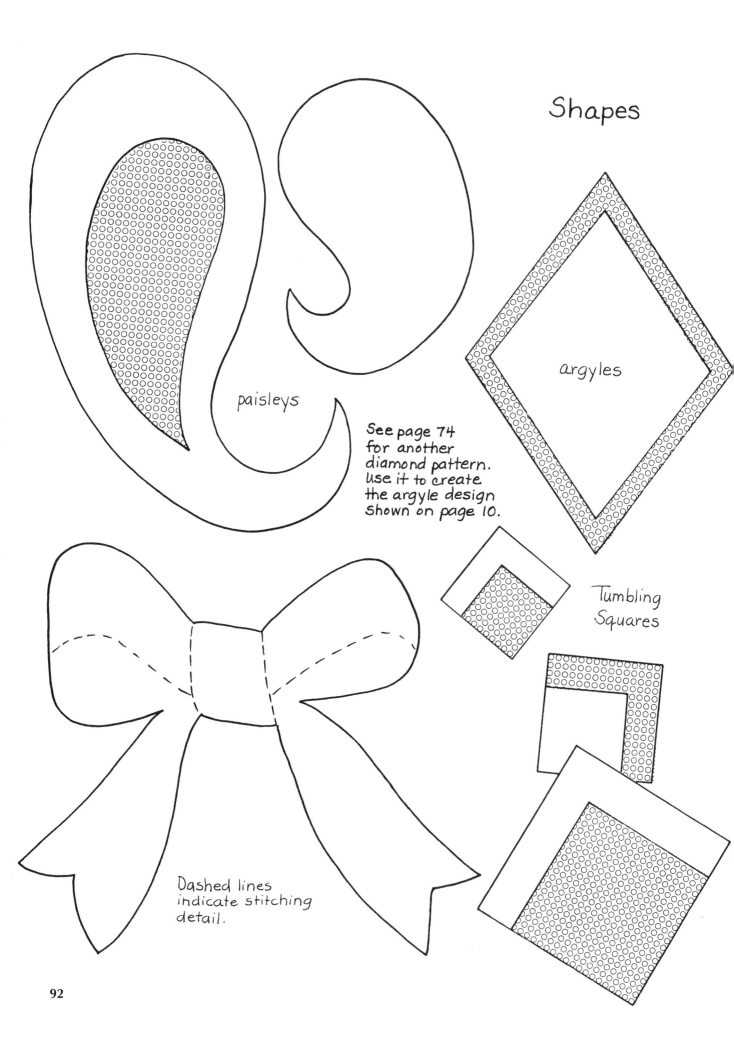

Shapes

paisleys

argyles

See page 74 for another diamond pattern. Use it to create the argyle design shown on page 10.

Tumbling Squares

Dashed lines indicate stitching detail.

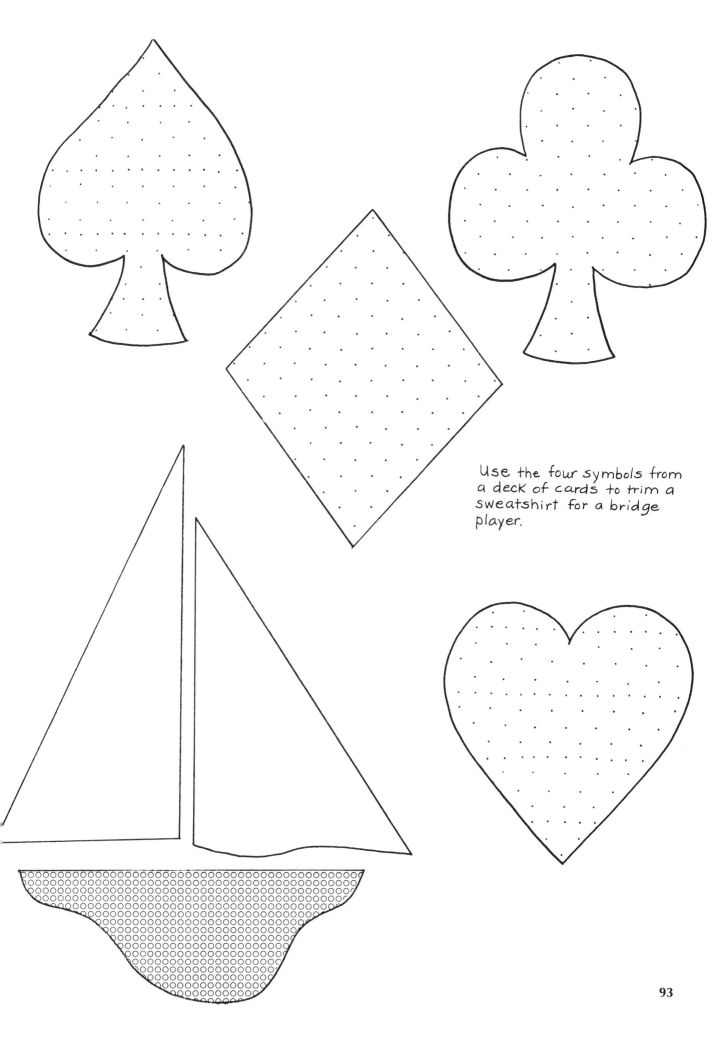

Use the four symbols from a deck of cards to trim a sweatshirt for a bridge player.

Butterflies

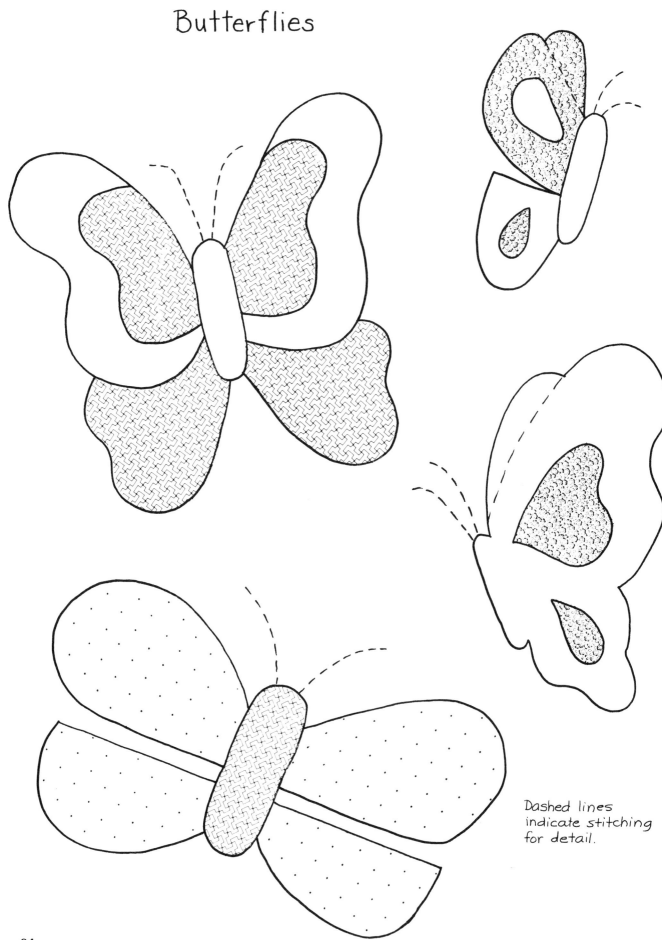

Dashed lines
indicate stitching
for detail.

94

Use a button, as shown, or a circle of fabric for the center of the flower.

95

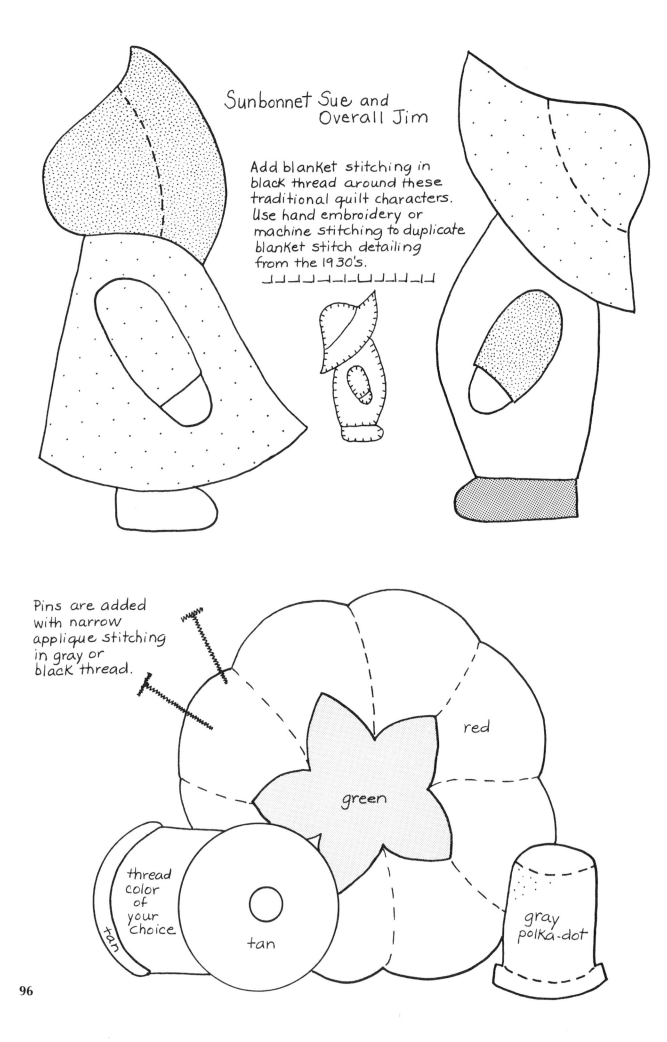

Sunbonnet Sue and
Overall Jim

Add blanket stitching in
black thread around these
traditional quilt characters.
Use hand embroidery or
machine stitching to duplicate
blanket stitch detailing
from the 1930's.

Pins are added
with narrow
applique stitching
in gray or
black thread.

red

green

thread
color
of
your
choice

tan

tan

gray
polka-dot

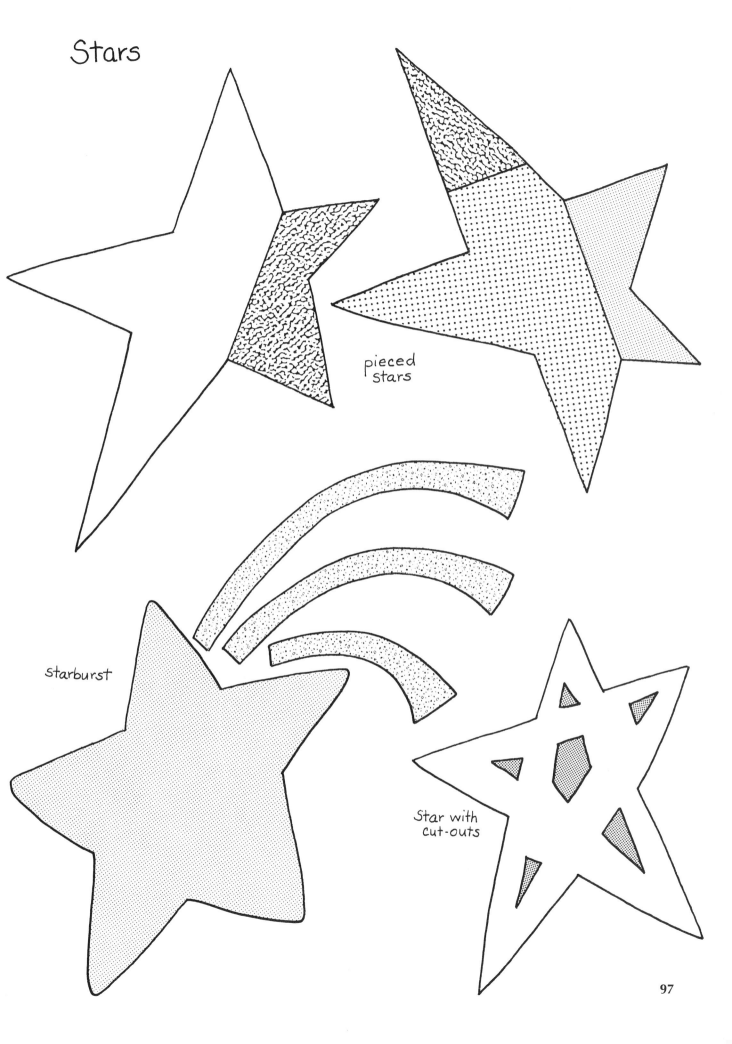

Stars

pieced
stars

starburst

Star with
cut-outs

97

Celebrations

Combine these designs for birthday, anniversary, or special events sweatshirts.

Use crystals, rhinestones, or sequins to represent bubbly champagne.

Angular Flowers and Leaves

Teacher Appliques

Designs are backward to make it easier for you to trace them onto paper-backed fusible web.

little red schoolhouse

Place designs in 4" squares divided by decorative machine stitching or narrow braid sewed onto the shirt.

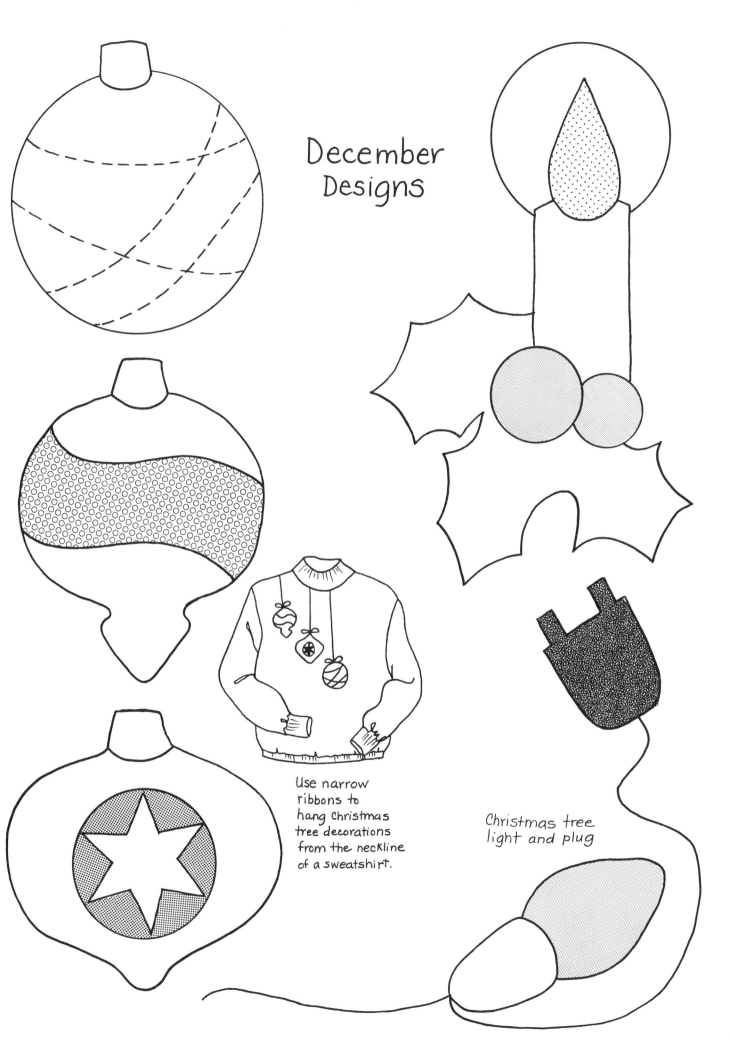

December Designs

Use narrow ribbons to hang christmas tree decorations from the neckline of a sweatshirt.

Christmas tree light and plug

Alphabet

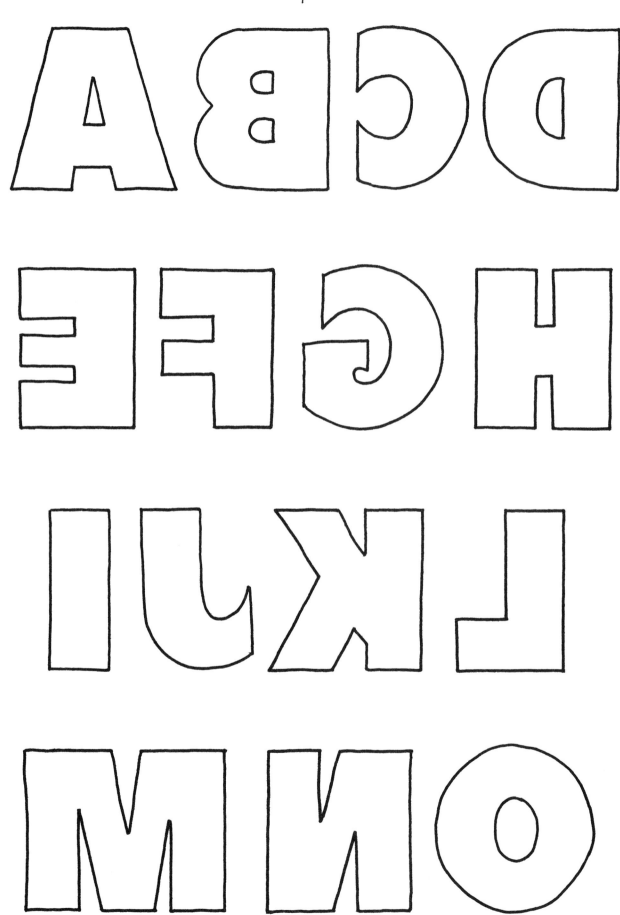

Alphabet letters are
printed backwards for
ease in tracing onto
paper-backed fusible
web for applique.

BIBLIOGRAPHY

Bradkin, Cheryl Greider. *Basic Seminole Patchwork*. Mountain View, CA: Leone Publications, 1990.

Fanning, Robbie and Tony. *The Complete Book of Machine Embroidery*. Radnor, PA: Chilton Book Company, 1986.

Hargrave, Harriet. *Mastering Machine Applique*. Lafayette, CA: C & T Publishing, 1991.

Mashuta, Mary. *Wearable Art for Real People*. Martinez, CA: C & T Publishing, 1989.

Mulari, Mary. *Adventure in Applique*. Aurora, MN: Mary's Productions, 1989.

Mulari, Mary. *Deluxe Designs*. Aurora, MN: Mary's Productions, 1992.

Ward, Nancy, *Fabric Painting Made Easy*. Radnor, PA: Chilton Book Company, 1993.

Zieman, Nancy. *10–20–30 Minutes to Sew*. Birmingham, AL: Oxmoor House, 1992.

Zieman, Nancy. *Let's Sew*. Beaver Dam, WI: Nancy's Notions, 1991.

SUPPLY RESOURCE LIST

Aardvark Adventures in Handicrafts
P.O. Box 2449
Livermore, CA 94551
*Threads and many wonderful,
unusual embellishments for
sweatshirts*

Alpha Shirt Company
401 East Hunting Park Avenue
Philadelphia, PA 19124
Blank sweatshirts by mail order

Cherrywood Quilts and Fabrics
361 Cherrywood Drive N.
Baxter, MN 56401
Hand-dyed cotton fabrics

Clotilde, Inc.
2 Sew Smart Way
B8031
Stevens Point, WI 54481-8031
Sewing notions mail-order catalog

Collars by Audrey
1211 Park Street
Alameda, CA 94501
*Knit collars and other products
by mail order*

Creative Crystals
P.O. Box 1232
Burlington, CT 06013
*Iron-on Austrian crystal
rhinestones and trims*

Keepsake Quilting
Route 25—P.O. Box 1618
Centre Harbor, NH 03226
*Cotton fabrics and sewing
notions mail-order catalog*

Marianne's Textile Products
Box 319, Rd. 2
Rockwood, PA 15557
Knit collars by mail order

Nancy's Notions
Box 683
Beaver Dam, WI 53916
Sewing notions mail-order catalog

Speed Stitch
3113-D Broadpoint Drive
Harbor Heights, FL 33983
*Decorative threads and sewing
supplies by mail order*

Stretch & Sew
19725 40th Avenue W
Suite G
Lynnwood, WA 98036
*Knit collars and fabrics by mail
order*

Treadleart
25834 Narbonne Avenue
Lomita, CA 90717
Sewing notions mail-order catalog

INDEX

ABOUT MARY MULARI

After years of searching for the right job, Mary Mulari discovered it at her fingertips. Always an avid sewer, Mary found her niche designing appliques and self-publishing creative sewing books.

While attending a craft show in 1982, she recalls, "I noticed several decorated sweatshirts at the show and realized how valuable these soft, warm garments are in our wardrobes." She experimented with sweatshirt decorations and began teaching a class on her discoveries for local community education. Since then, she has been teaching and sharing her ideas at seminars around the United States and publishing books. As her following continues to grow, her decorating techniques are making their way onto a variety of garments in addition to sweatshirts.

Designer Sweatshirts, her first book, proved so successful that in 1984 Mulari published a second book, *Applique Design Collection.* These were followed by six other books: *More Designer Sweatshirts, Country Style Appliques, Adventure in Applique, Accents for Your Style, Designer Wearables and Gifts,* and *Deluxe Designs.* In addition, she has designed a collection of notecards with sewing designs and produced a 60-minute video based on her first sweatshirt book.

Mary Mulari is proud to say that she learned to sew as a member of the Loon Lake 4-H Club. She has a bachelor of science degree in English education from the University of Minnesota, Duluth. A resident of Aurora, Minnesota, Mary and her husband, Barry, own a retail sporting goods and clothing business. Her designs and writing have appeared in several publications, including *Woman's World, Workbasket, Wearable Wonders,* and *Sewing Update Newsletter.* She has made frequent appearances on the television series "Sewing with Nancy" and was a guest on the PBS television series, "Creative Living with Sheryl Borden." She continues to develop ideas for new publications, to market her books, and to teach seminars.

By using her talents and creativeness in sewing, designing, and writing, Mary Mulari truly has found her work at her fingertips.

Mary Mulari appreciates comments, questions, and ideas from her readers. You may write to her at: Box 87-Dept.SWS, Aurora, MN 55705